GIFT OF

The Dark
Angel

GIFT OF
The Dark
Angel

*A Woman's
Journey through
Depression toward
Wholeness*

BY ANN KEIFFER

With Foreword by Judith Duerk,
author of *Circle of Stones*

San Diego, California

LURAMEDIA ™

LuraMedia
7060 Miramar Road, Suite 104
San Diego, CA 92121

Library of Congress Cataloging-in-Publication Data

Keiffer, Ann, date.
    Gift of the dark angel : a woman's journey through depression
    toward wholeness / by Ann Keiffer.
        p.   cm.
    ISBN 0-931055-85-7
    1. Keiffer, Ann, date.   —Mental health.   2. Depression,
    Mental—Patients—United States—Biography.   I. Title.
    [RC537.K44A3   1991]
    616.85'27'0092—dc20
    [B]   91-23526
                                                              CIP

Grateful acknowledgment is made to the following copyright
holders for permission to use their copyrighted material:

LuraMedia, for the quotations from CIRCLE OF STONES by Judith
        Duerk, © copyright 1989 by LuraMedia.
Oxford University Press, for the quotation reprinted from
        CHRISTIAN DISCOURSES by Soren Kierkegaard, © copyright
        1939. By permission of Oxford University Press.
Scripture quotations are from the Revised Standard Version Bible,
        copyright 1946, 1952, 1971 by the Division of Christian
        Education of National Council of Churches of Christ in the
        USA. Used by permission.

The events depicted in this book are true.
The names of certain people and
organizations have been changed.

Acknowledgments

*T*o all of the people who made this book possible, I give my deep and heartfelt thanks. To Carla and Tom Gerber, Dulcie Andres, and Lorna Carparelli who urged me to write my story and were my trusted first readers. To Alfred Fricke, Ph.D., for his wisdom and wit, for his support during my depression, and for his professional review of the material in the manuscript dealing with my therapy. To Melvin Friedman, D.O., for his personal interest in this project and for his professional review of medical references in the manuscript. And most of all, to Larry, my wonderful husband, who has loved me so; through him I have known a glimpse of God.

To my well-loved father,
who went before
and did the best he could.
May this be your healing, too.

And Jacob was left alone; and a man wrestled with him until the breaking of the day. When the man saw that he did not prevail against Jacob, he touched the hollow of his thigh; and Jacob's thigh was put out of joint as he wrestled with him. Then he said, "Let me go, for the day is breaking." But Jacob said, "I will not let you go, unless you bless me." And he said to him, "What is your name?" And he said, "Jacob." Then he said, "Your name shall no more be called Jacob, but Israel, for you have striven with God and with men, and have prevailed." Then Jacob asked him, "Tell me, I pray, your name." But he said, "Why is it that you ask my name?" And there he blessed him. So Jacob called the name of the place Peniel, saying, "For I have seen God face to face, and yet my life is preserved."

Genesis 32: 24-30, RSV

Contents

Preface

*T*hrough the miracle of synchronicity, one month after I had completed the original manuscript for this book, Judith Duerk's book, *Circle of Stones: Woman's Journey to Herself*, came into my hands. My heart leapt to find a therapist writing about women's depression from a point of view that so matched my own experience and writing in such a beautiful and moving way. I was so touched by the spirit of *Circle of Stones* that I rewrote portions of my manuscript to include quotes from Judith Duerk. With synchronicity at work again, Judith Duerk's publisher, LuraMedia, was eventually to become my publisher, too. I thank Judith Duerk both for *Circle of Stones* and for the Foreword she has written for *Gift of the Dark Angel*.

Foreword

by Judith Duerk

$\mathcal{H}$ardly anything in contemporary society is as deeply feared as depression. Our culture places great value on competitiveness and success. Much energy is given to outer appearances and little to the inner life of the individual. We are frantic to get ahead and often suppress our feeling needs, at great cost. Depression is the insistence of our inner nature that we come into a more honest balance. Like the dragon hiding behind the mountain, it is hardly mentioned and rarely dealt with.

Ann Keiffer draws our respect as a remarkable exception and an encouraging example. Ann lived with awareness through a depression that lasted several years. She allowed herself to experience it, rather than rising above it, worked with it until it offered up its truth for her life. The Dark Angel visited Ann during her late thirties. It came — as it always does, uninvited — into a life that seemed to be successful in every way.

Ann's pattern had been to expect a great deal of herself. Like many women of today, she gave herself away many times, not realizing that she was pushing herself far past her own limits. As a child, she had fulfilled every expectation placed upon her. Ann could see, later, that she had internalized very early that "life was about achievement."

When the first dark shadows of the Angel's wings drifted across her life, Ann was able to continue her work without recognizing them. A bright and energetic mode covered her fatigue. She managed always to cope by pushing herself a little harder.

Finally, she could no longer deny the Gift the Dark Angel brought. A deep depression enveloped her, brought her outer life to a stop. Ann was pulled into an abyss, a desolation so total that she wondered if she would survive.

Ann describes poignantly her sense of shame and inadequacy during this time and her railing against her own condition. She became painfully aware of how forbidden depression is in our society. Her life became even more difficult as former associates were unable to reach out in a convincing way. Their doubts and fears made Ann's isolation complete.

Alone, at the bottom of the abyss, she waited.

At last, Ann received true witnessing, and her pain was validated. There was a turning. Like many women of today, Ann realized that she must bring into new balance her needs in the Masculine and Feminine realms.

As she worked with this, with the values of Doing and Being, she came to new awareness of her needs in the Feminine realm — her need for quiet, for time alone, time in nature, time to Be. She began, slowly, to restructure her life, moment by moment, allowing these needs to be the center, rather than the periphery.

Ann had the faith to believe that there was meaning in her depression and the courage to write about it in her own subjective terms, sharing that meaning with others. The Dark Angel visited Ann Keiffer and brought Ann the Gift of herself.

Judith Duerk,
therapist and
author of CIRCLE OF STONES

1

Lighting the Lamp

$\mathcal{W}$hen I was thirty-six years old, I had it made.

Two years before, I'd given up my regular paycheck to chase down a chance at a dream. More than anything, I'd wanted to become an advertising copywriter. By the time I was thirty-six, without any formal training and by the skin of my own wits, I'd pulled it off. *More* than pulled it off — I'd gotten myself hired by one of the best ad agencies in the business. I was full of enthusiasm and the joy of life, higher than the cow that jumped over the moon. On top of this, I had an adoring husband and a terrific teenage son. If not the Queen of Hearts and Happiness, I felt, at the very least, like a princess in line to the throne.

When I was thirty-eight, without warning, I plummeted into the deepest black abyss of depression — an abyss as desolate and final as a grave. Alone, at the bottom of that grave, I struggled with the Dark Angel of depression for more than a year. I was deadened by fatigue, sick and spiritless, so brain-weary even the smallest decisions overwhelmed me. Though I wept for want of sleep, I could not rest. Though I hungered for health, I could not eat. I lost hope, lost my way, lost myself, and finally lost all reason to live.

Why did this depression fell me? By what means was I resurrected from it? Why do I now consider my sojourn in hell both a grace and a blessing? In the beginning I thought these questions were a matter only for my own personal catechism. But I now believe that my story, the meaning and soul-direction I found buried in my depression, may have significance for other people, too. Especially other women.

When I was in my late twenties, I had a Technicolor dream that hinted strongly of an inner conflict, and the dream has remained straight-pinned to my memory for years:

> *I am planning to sew some new clothes for myself. I have purchased a crisp cotton fabric, woven in a cheerful plaid of Crayola hues: chartreuse, yellow, hot pink, and orange. The fabric is laid out on the table, but I am confused. The only pattern I own is for a man's suit, and I am disturbed because I have forgotten the tricks I used to know that would make a man's suit fit me.*

I knew this dream was important. I even suspected it was a kind of warning — that my fabric wasn't suited to a pattern meant for a man, that I was at risk for making a life that did not fit me. But what *was* the masculine pattern of which the dream warned? I was petite, at ease in relationships, cooperative, and easily competent — in what way was I a masculine woman? Too young and too early bent, I did not recognize that my basic operating principle — my relentless drive to "make things happen," my incessant "doing" and striving — was a masculine value. And I had no idea how little I valued or understood my own feminine soul.

Shortly after my man's-suit dream, I was attending a seminar in which we were introduced to a technique called "active imagination," a process whereby imagination could be employed to solve problems, encourage relaxation, and provide insightful guidance. With our eyes closed, we were asked to imagine for ourselves "a safe place," a place where we could retreat when we needed to seek our own answers. This safe place was to have two doors. And on that day, each of those two doors was to open in turn, revealing someone with whom we needed to communicate.

For my safe place I built a room paneled in redwood, hung it with ferns as befit the 1960s, and installed two doors which, for some reason, rose slowly from bottom to top. But I was not prepared for the two people who arrived:

The door on the right side of my safe place slowly rises. I see a pair of black, threatening, sharp-toed cowboy boots, followed by black pants and a black silk shirt with three of its buttons left undone to reveal a chestful of gold chains and medallions. Here he is: a handsome gunslinger with jet-black hair, a black hat, and a villain's thin black mustache. His name is Duke. He doesn't walk; he swaggers. A bar-brawler, a guy who drives a car like a weapon, Duke radiates raw masculine power — a power which, in his case, is twisted by a mean spirit.

It was not the first time I had seen Duke. I had already met him once before in a dream — a dream in which he was menacing a woman, threatening to torture her, pinning her to the ground with one black boot placed on her chest. And I was the woman in that dream.

Duke was the opposite of any man I ever would have wanted to know. In fact, I would have walked through a sewer to avoid any man like him. Still, I found myself inexplicably drawn to him, mesmerized by his ruthlessness and power. Duke, I later realized, was the representation of my own inner masculine values, the force that drove me to do and achieve. And when I abdicated my authority to him, Duke was the force that became my *un*doing.

When the door on the left side of my safe place rose, it revealed a person who was Duke's opposite in every way:

The first thing I see is a pair of dirty feet with broken toenails and the callouses of hard-traveling. Incongruously, as the door rises higher, I see the skirt of a pink satin, tiered dress, one very like a dress I wore when I played the part of a dancing doll in an operetta when I was a little girl. But, in this case, the dress belongs to a woman.

As the door continues to rise slowly all the way to the top, I see beautiful, womanly hands, and then a long strand of pearls looping down from a slender neck. Finally, I am looking on the wavy, golden hair of a Southern belle and the pretty, but despairing, face of Valentine.

For that was her name. I knew it surely. Just as I knew that she represented my own inner feminine. But what was the meaning of those dirty, hardened feet? And why was she so sad? Unfortunately, Valentine would become sadder still — and very sick — before I would actually come to appreciate her value. The healing of Valentine would be my own healing.

In her book, *Circle of Stones*, Judith Duerk, a therapist with a Jungian perspective, writes:

> Collective attitudes have evolved fostering archetypal masculine doing and achieving values. As woman entered the work realm outside her home. . . . There was little recognition that her process as a woman was of a different nature or that doing/achievement values were not complete or valid for her.
>
> The issue is not whether a woman can achieve, but that preoccupation with achievement may deny a descent into her deeper nature which a woman must make to touch her true strengths . . . the power of the feminine . . . comes of *being*, not *doing* . . .[1]

How might such a compulsion toward doing and achieving — and our reluctance to put value on reflection, quiet time, and introversion — relate to the fact that twenty-five percent of all women in the United States will go through a depression sometime during their lives?[2] How might such a compulsion relate to my own depression? Judith Duerk goes on to describe what may happen if we, as women, allow ourselves to become driven in our pursuit of achievement, mere slaves to a daily onslaught of tasks and busy-ness:

If a woman is caught in overextended lifestyle and achievement-oriented values, depression or illness may offer the only opportunity to allow her to be with herself. As she ignores her own needs for quiet and self-nurture, the voice of the deeper Self may call through depression. If a woman cannot let herself hear her own needs, but continues to adhere fearfully to a lifestyle that denies her inner growth and deepening, the voice of the Self may manifest in physical illness as the only possible way to force her to take time to be with herself.[3]

Into such a life, Duerk says, "depression comes as a gift, bringing the chance to strike root in a deeper ground inside oneself."[4]

But depression comes as a perilous gift, one so perilous it is rarely recognized as a gift at all. Whatever the cause — genetics, grief, isolation, family problems, illness, trauma, or the stress of an overextended lifestyle — depression is so repellent that most of us shrink from it and thrust it away. Most of us have been taught to fear depression in ourselves, and in others. And, if we are struck down by it, we know of only three options: fight it, deny it, or succumb.

Initially, I believed that fighting my depression was the only way I could survive. For months I grasped at a ragged hope that I could somehow escape from my struggle with the Dark Angel, put a tourniquet on my sorrow, and crawl, grope my way back to what I thought of as "normal life."

In all my thirty-eight years, I had known no other woman — nor any man — who had gone into that blackness and come out of it renewed. Or, perhaps more accurately, I had no way of telling if someone had. In our society most people are hesitant to talk about their dark nights of the soul in day-to-day conversation. And since our most profound experiences are rarely discussed, we end up none the wiser. We lose the comfort we might gain from another's experience, the reassurance a knowing traveler could give us that the journey through depression has meaning, that there are treasures in the abyss.

I have been to the bottom of the abyss, and I can tell you: The black cavern of depression is shot with veins of copper, silver, gold, even diamonds — the treasure of creative new meaning for our lives. But to mine these treasures, we must have courage, the courage to descend into that blackness and inch along in a painstaking exploration of our own uncharted depths.

This is the story of such a descent. In the telling of it, I will take you down into the abyss of my depression with the truest words I can find. And I will leave nothing out— not the chaos of the fall, the deadening despair, nor the love that was a candle in my darkness.

But I cannot begin this story with a woman teetering on the brink of depression. The roots of this depression twine down into the very ground of my being. To understand why I ended up tumbling into my own private hell, you'll need to know something about the girl I once was, the family from which I came, the inner forces that drove me. It's all reflected in five photos I've pulled from the family album:

———

School Days, 1951:
This is my first-grade picture, a hand-tinted photo, with Scotch tape yellowing at the corners now. I have a heart-shaped face, wide-set blue eyes, and a nipped nose. My hair is blonde, parted on the side with springy pincurls, and my bangs are cut up-to-here. I'm wearing a homemade dress and a broad, forced smile.

Underneath the photo my mother has written, "School gave Ann the stomachache because she always *tried so hard.*" In fact, I was so terrified I'd fail in my schoolwork, I gagged repeatedly and threw up in the front yard every single morning for weeks. At six, my stomach and I already knew that life was about achieving.

———

Easter Sunday, 1958:
When I was thirteen, I took this snapshot of my brothers and sisters — Bobby, eleven; Tina, nine; Frank, seven; and Molly, four. They're posing, almost cooperatively, on the front steps of the white-framed church in my hometown. We live in Nankin, Ohio, a don't-blink village of about thirty houses laid out on dirt streets, our only amenities, besides the church, an old gas station, a brick schoolhouse, and a combination volunteer fire department/post office. My mother has been busy; look at those scrubbed and smiling faces, the polished shoes, my brothers' fresh burr haircuts, my sisters' shining hair and new Easter dresses.

I was the oldest of all the Brownson kids and took that responsibility seriously. I realized early that my job was to be good, set a good example, and work hard to please. And I was very good at my job. I never met a line I couldn't toe.

———

My Mother's Yearbook Photo:
At seventeen, in her senior picture, my mother is wearing a simple black sweater and a single strand of simulated pearls. She is the proverbially beautiful

farmer's daughter — long chestnut hair, blue eyes, and apple-polished innocence. But actually, in her heyday, my mother was more her father's son — slinging bales, pitching hay, milking cows, learning that the measure of her self-worth could be computed precisely and completely by how much she could accomplish and how hard she could work.

Once, in fifth grade, I inadvertently failed to measure up to my mother's hard-work ethic. Each week, student volunteers worked in the cafeteria in exchange for a week of free lunches. By turn, volunteers served food, wiped tables, punched lunch tickets, passed out milk and straws, and scraped dirty trays. I loved to volunteer, but one day the cooks overhead me say I liked serving food the best and scraping trays the least. This got back to my mother as gossip. She told me she was ashamed of me, that she wanted me to be known as a "good worker." From that day on, I scraped trays symbolically and unceasingly everywhere I went — in classrooms, at home, in workplaces — always trying to prove what was already so: I was a good worker.

My mother was the instant bonding glue that held all our lives together, though she often seemed too busy to notice anything beyond meals, laundry, babies, and baths . . . and the fact that she had no college diploma hanging on the wall next to dad's.

I admired my mother, counted on her, was comforted by her care, loved her, but I misunderstood. What I, for years, saw as her stoicism, her steel-coiled strength, I now know was a shield for a vulnerability too fragile to make public.

————

Sports Page Photo of My Father:
*The man shaking hands and accepting the trophy in
this newspaper clipping is my father; he's just been
named Coach of the Year for the state of Ohio, an honor
he won four times. He was a football coach. A maker of
champions. A mercurial, gifted man with a quick wit
who achieved great things too early. And died young, at
fifty-two, leaving to us, his family, echoes of laughter,
and a brooding, uneasy shadow.*

Sometimes I think the word "charisma" was invented
just for my dad. His fiery talks in the locker room were
legend. At the half time of one game, my father worked his
team into such a competitive frenzy they *stampeded* back
on the field, smashing the metal locker room door right off
its hinges before anyone had time to open it. When I grew
up, I wanted to be as strong as those football players and as
powerful as my father.

One of my fondest memories is of my handsome, dark-
haired father doing a recklessly happy dance in the kitchen
one payday, tucking a folded twenty-dollar bill down my
mother's cleavage as she stood at the dishpan, with soap-
suds up to her elbows, laughing.

One of my saddest memories is of my father years
later, tipped back in his recliner — a wasted, sallow ache of
a man, sitting in the dark — dying of ill health, self-
loathing, and brutal depression. The saying goes "like father, like *son*," but now a daughter wonders.

————

Our Wedding Day, 1966:
This candid shot captures the bride and groom deep in a private kiss in front of one of the milky cream-and-green stained-glass windows in the Nankin Federated Church. I am holding onto my satin headpiece and veil in the wedding dress my mother made. Larry — slim, dark-haired, his eyes framed by serious horn-rimmed glasses — is somehow military-looking in his rented morning coat — an officer and a gentle man, bending down to embrace me and put his lips on mine.

To us, it had seemed a long aisle to the altar. Larry and I met when I was a senior in high school, and he was a sophomore at Purdue University. I knew immediately that Larry was special — a White Knight — and we steady-dated summers and long distance for the next year-and-a-half. However, by the time I was a sophomore in college, I was becoming disenchanted. Suddenly Larry seemed like *too much* of a nice guy; I had in mind someone who was more exciting, slightly outrageous, someone who would dance my shoes off. When we split up, Larry told his mother, "If I can't have Ann, I don't want anyone."

For the next seven months I dated a few Dark Knights and began to realize what I had honored in Larry — his integrity, his sincerity, the gentleness of his masculinity, his wholehearted willingness to love. Finally, I called him and asked if we could give our relationship one more chance, and very soon the two of us began to braid our lives together again. We were married as soon as Larry finished graduate school and I completed everything for my degree in elementary education except student teaching.

I can tell you now, without question, that Larry proved to be the White Knight I always thought he was. When I most needed order, constancy, and faith, Larry was there with all that and a gift ten thousand times more precious and rare: love that was unconditional. When this man made the vow "in sickness and in health," he meant it. I know. Because in 1983 he was tested.

———

Now, at last, armed with this information, we are ready. Strike a match. Light your lamp. The journey begins.

2

Grist for the Big-Time Daily Grind

$\mathcal{B}$y the year 1979, the year my pursuit of achievement began to spiral out of control, there had been a lot of water, chalk dust, and mother's milk under the bridge.

In 1966, immediately after our wedding, Larry and I moved to King of Prussia, Pennsylvania, where Larry was employed by the General Electric Space Technology Center, and I began my career as an elementary school teacher. We had planned to stay in the East, but in 1969 Larry's career path detoured him — and us — way out to Sunnyvale, California, the home of Lockheed Missiles and Space Company.

Frankly, California wasn't my first choice of places to live, but the tight job market Larry was facing left us no choice. For starters, I didn't look forward to the move because I was five months pregnant, and I regretted leaving both of our families three thousand miles behind in Ohio. More than that, I couldn't imagine fitting into the California lifestyle which, in my mind, consisted of sweltering under plastic palm trees, blinking back the neon nights, and driving around with wind-swept brains in convertibles.

However, as soon as our plane hit the runway at San Francisco International Airport, I was a convert. California — Northern California, at least — was nothing like I had expected.

California! I wanted to throw my arms around the rugged peaks of her mountains, roll down her golden hills. I loved San Francisco, the Bay, the Golden Gate, the air, the sunlight washing translucent over pastel-painted homes and shimmering in groves of redwoods.

After four months of furious nest-making in our townhouse in Sunnyvale, that December Larry and I were blessed with the birth of a beautiful, healthy son, John. However, my life did not seem to be turning out quite as I'd expected. The birth of my first child was also the birth of my last . . .

John's delivery was grievously mismanaged by my obstetrician and, seven days later, because of the doctor's errors, I suffered a massive hemorrhage. As the paramedics rushed me from my home on a stretcher, zipped up to my neck in a rubber body bag slippery with my own blood, I was sure I would never see my baby or another day again. All my girlish dreams of a cottage in the woods complete with a picket fence, a rose arbor, four beautiful children, and endless sunshine were cast forever into shadow by the very real specter of death.

Because of the toll this trauma took and permanent physical problems related to my pregnancy, Larry and I decided John would be our only child. I had no passion to go back to teaching and, since John was to be our darling one-and-only, I decided I wanted to be a full-time mom during his preschool years. So we wrapped John's baby and toddler years in bright-colored bunting — trips to the park, endless sessions of chasing and giggling, a million kisses and hugs, bedtime stories with lots of snuggling, co-op nursery school — we had it all. Together.

I counted those years I had at home with John a privilege. But, by 1973 when John was four, I was coming down with a bad case of cabin fever. While I was an expert at keeping myself busy, doing, doing, doing — laundry, cooking, cleaning — I began to wish for something more interesting in my life than mere household routines. Fortunately, two of my friends were feeling the same way. Out of our mutual need for stimulation and gainful employment — with no connections, zero capital, and so little experience we didn't know a P.O. (purchase order) from an AT&T — we began designing and wholesaling children's screen-printed T-shirts.

However, T-shirts didn't satisfy my cravings for action long, either. In 1979 I left the business — but not my friends — and talked my way into an even more exciting job: working as personal assistant to an outrageously funny, handsome, tart-tongued, dress-for-success consultant in San Francisco. This job really opened doors for me: the doors to I. Magnin, expensive San Francisco boutiques, and shops on Rodeo Drive in Los Angeles. Not that I bought anything in the glitzier places. But the little girl who had shopped at small-town JCPenney stores all her life gradually became a woman who could look at the triple-digit price tag on a silk blouse without hyperventilating.

After just nine months, almost certain now that my attention span for careers was impaired, I quit my dress-for-success job and went stalking an even bigger challenge. At that point in my search for a career, there were only two things I knew for sure: I still wasn't being what I wanted to be when I grew up, and I didn't have a clue what that was.

So that's where I began; I temporarily became a highly motivated, full-time career counselor for myself. In pouring over books at the public library, I came across a career guidebook that contained specific skills assessment exercises. As I worked through each of the exercises, a pattern began to emerge. Most of my skills fell into two categories: influencing/persuading skills and language/reading/writing/speaking skills. Suddenly it came to me what I wanted to be when I grew up. *Ann,* I said to myself, *you should be writing for advertisers!*

Wow, what an exciting career advertising would be! But I didn't want to go back to college. I wondered, could I become an advertising writer without getting another degree? Since there was no one around to tell me the truth — that it could not be done; that advertising was an elitist business reserved only for the best and the brightest, the hard-driving, and the slightly bent; that you got your degree for starters and then worked your way up from the anonymity of the mailroom — I forged ahead, with John and Larry cheering me on with choruses of "Go for it!" I think it was right about then that I let my Duke-self climb up on his black stallion and take complete control of the reins of my life. Oh, I would go for it, all right!

Undeterred by my lack of experience, a degree, or a

mentor, I launched my attack on the citadel of advertising, specifically direct marketing. Direct marketing advertising seemed exactly the kind of challenge I'd always sought. I thought if I could inspire people to get up out of their chairs to call an 800 number or mail in a response card or order NOW, surely I could write *any* kind of advertising.

But where to start? I promptly went back to the library and read my way through all the direct marketing advertising books in the stacks. Once I'd accomplished that, I ordered more books by mail and read those, too. Could I teach myself to be an ad writer? I could and I did — in spades. After free-lancing for just a year-and-a-half, I got myself hired by the direct marketing division of Lawrence & Buckingham (L&B), one of the top four advertising agencies in the world.

Do these sound like the actions of a marked woman, a passive, poor soul destined for depression? Not at all. I was a woman at the zenith of triumph. How willingly and gladly I threw myself between the great grinding stones of big-time advertising! Landing this job was the most thrilling thing that had ever happened to me. However, I was also pee-in-my-pants scared . . .

Here I was, a compulsive achiever and the greenest of greenhorns at the same time. I was terrified someone at L&B would realize I was a kid from Ohio who'd landed in the big-time by mistake, a ringer who should be booted out the door. I frantically searched for the line at L&B so I could toe it . . . but the line seemed as arbitrary as it was invisible.

Since Stephen Katz, the Creative Director (CD) at L&B had hired me, he'd obviously seen some glimmer of talent. But he also had more reservations than Pan Am. On my first day at the job, he called me into his office to "welcome" me.

"Okay," Stephen said, "I'm giving you a shot at this. But you've got just six months to prove yourself. If you don't work out, you're out the door. No hard feelings."

A trial period was certainly reasonable. Also stab-in-the-heart stressful. I felt as if I were back in grade school again; I tried so hard my stomach ached every day. For those next few months, my six-month trial hung over my head like a safe suspended on a thread thirty stories up.

It was Jim who finally held me up so I could pin my star in the sky. A pro who'd given up a CD job across town so he could get back in front of a typewriter, Jim became the friend and mentor I so desperately needed. From him I learned to trust my instincts and quit worrying about "doing it right." I wrote from my gut and my heart, and once I began to pour myself out on the page like that, my copy broke response records. I won awards. Clients were elated. I was good. Damn good. How I loved that job and my life!

But no matter how confident I became, the job never seemed to get easier. In the L&B office stress hung in the air like a haze of coal soot — a combination of everyone's personal burn-out and the ever-smoldering combustion between Stephen and Franklin, L&B's Managing Director. The two men hated each other to the bone.

One would have thought that, over time, Stephen would have learned to forgive Franklin's tendency to goose-step and issue marching orders; and Franklin, to trust Stephen to come through with blockbuster creative work in his own sweet, maddening, procrastinating time. But it didn't happen. Instead, their guerilla warfare erupted in a bloody coup . . .

Stephen had just boarded a plane for a vacation in Mexico when Franklin dropped the bomb: Stephen, he told the staff, was fired as-of-now. Personally, I didn't know whether to cheer or shed tears. I felt loyal to Stephen; after all, he'd given me the biggest break of my life. When his "having a nice time" postcards arrived from Mexico, I was anguished by his innocence. But I also wasn't looking forward to his coming back. Stephen's procrastination and aloofness were aggravating to those of us on his creative team, too. And none of us enjoyed watching Stephen and Franklin seethe, covertly cheer each other's misfortunes, and sharpen their wits on one another, aiming to draw blood.

Stephen, not having a clue, agreed to meet Franklin for dinner on the Sunday night before his supposed return to work, and that's when Franklin laid the news on him that he'd been fired. Angry, unintentionally creating a situation so awkward it was all thumbs and elbows, Stephen refused to accept his dismissal and came to work anyway! With perfect logic, faith in himself and the L&B organization, he believed he could appeal the firing to management in New York and be reinstated. But he was not reinstated.

Stephen's firing-in-absentia left all of us at the agency a little crazy. We were embarrassed for Stephen, for our own parts in his demise, and for a rotten business where you can go on vacation and your company can cut off your benefits and clean out your desk for you while you're gone. We were half afraid to leave our desks to go out and get food at noon. Who knew — you might not have a job when you got back.

Jack, our most seasoned veteran of the direct-marketing wars, was someone who wielded his experience like a field marshal wields his swagger stick. We used to razz him about the way he tried to haul out his dusty, old arthritic rules to whack the creatives into line at strategy meetings.

Jack wore zip-up boots made in England, custom-tailored pin-striped suits, and a bandito mustache. He earned my devotion forever when I walked in the door one day wearing my sunglasses and a white coat, and he hollered at me, "Hey, Hollywood!" For a full five minutes, I actually felt downright glamorous!

Like Stephen, Jack also sometimes chafed under Franklin's management, but he had a different way of dealing with it. He cultivated an amiable relationship with Franklin, worked hard, took no guff, and, when the timing was right, he simply took one of L&B's clients and went off to start his own agency.

Our next CD (or Queen of the Universe, as we sometimes called her) was Victoria. Possessing an extravagance of talent and good looks, Victoria ruled the L&B creative realm with an iron charm even Franklin found hard to duck or direct. A masterful presenter and a sharp business-woman, Victoria may have invented self-esteem, and she dressed the part; we rarely saw her wear the same outfit twice!

While Victoria exuded high-energy and good spirits, I never felt I could quite connect with her. Like a star you watch on TV every week, she seemed to be someone you knew well, but you didn't necessarily know her at all. To maintain her objectivity, Victoria erected a one-way screen of professionalism between herself and her employees. Onto that screen she projected only her public persona and, thank heavens, a very real warmth. But she never let anyone get behind that invisible protective shield of objec-tivity if she could help it.

Even with all this going on, these were still bright new shiny-penny days for me at L&B. Days of goofy coffee-room camaraderie, slam-dunk deadlines, high-output creativity, top-that witticisms, waterfall laughter, entertaining clients on sky's-the-limit expense accounts, raucous celebrations, triumphant wins of new business and plaques to hang on our walls, glorious days of toasting our success with Pepsi and champagne.

Yes, all those days I gave myself willingly and joyously to the stones as grist for the daily grind. So joyously and blindly did I give myself, I did not notice when the stones first began to destroy me. Did not notice even as I was slowly being reduced to a mere grit of crushed bone-and-spirit. Hard, pebbly grit, but grit so vulnerable and fine it might be blown to nothingness by a single breath.

3

The Body Never Lies

*I*t was the first week of February, 1983, a little more than two years after I'd started my job at L&B. My alarm rang. Red-eyed and jangled, I reached over to shut off the noise. It was jarringly unnecessary; I'd spent most of the night lying rigidly awake — a torment that was becoming habitual.

Gone were my new-kid-on-the-block days of airy jubilation at L&B. The atmosphere in the office was now so relentless, fast-paced, and stressful, we all joked about wishing we had a Valium dispenser in the coffee room. Though I still loved my job with a passion that was almost obscene, the Lord of Stress was beginning to exact his pound of flesh from me. However, I didn't realize that yet. I knew only that I was exhausted. So exhausted, my body felt as if it were weighed down with hundreds of pounds of chain-mail armor. And now my hands were on fire.

About two months earlier, a raging, fiery rash of hard red bumps had suddenly erupted in symmetrical patterns on both my hands — also my elbows, the back of my head, my knees, and my feet. At first the rash mysteriously appeared and disappeared, and then it was with me continually, like nettles sewn into my flesh. Nothing touched the furies of that fire. Not calamine; nor cortisone; nor gels, lotions, or potions; nor over-the-counter remedies of any kind.

This was an affliction worthy of Job but, unlike Job, I had no idea what the source of my affliction was. Because rending of garments, weeping and wailing, and gnashing of teeth were considered bad form in the offices of L&B, when I was at work I hid behind a happy face mask and dealt with the rash as unobtrusively as possible. At home, I admit, I did a little rending, wailing, and gnashing. But as bad as it was, I was determined to plow on. I kept my whip cracking over my own back at L&B while, at the same time, trying everything I could think of to put an end to my rash of misfortune.

At first, I just gritted my teeth and tried to wait out the rash. When that didn't work, I tried eliminating or changing chemicals that came in contact with my skin — fabric softeners, hand lotions, perfume, detergents, shampoos, and soaps. When that didn't work, I tried avoiding common food allergens — milk products, citrus, corn, eggs. Finally, I hypothesized our dog might have brought poison oak sap into the house on her coat. So I had the carpet cleaned and the dog bathed down to her scrawny little hide. But absolutely nothing helped; the conflagration under my skin raged on.

Ice was the only thing that kept me from screaming in frustration and itching my skin until it bled. At work I kept cups of ice cubes on my desk, or next to my chair at the conference table during business meetings. Every few minutes — when I couldn't bear the itching any longer — I'd palm an ice cube and sneak it out of sight under the desk or table. Then, in semisecret, I would rub the ice on my fiery hands and feet until the itching subsided enough that I could concentrate on the work in front of me once again. It was not easy to be upbeat, witty, and creative above the desk or table when I was in agony below. But I loved that job, and I wasn't going to let some miserable rash bump me from my coveted rung on the corporate ladder.

However, by February it was obvious the rash wasn't a simple problem of a wayward weed or a fleeting chemical reaction. I was going to need medical attention. Though I hated to take the time off work, this particular Wednesday morning in February I had an appointment to see a doctor — someone I hoped would know how to end my irritation once and for all.

I dragged myself out of bed that morning and showered in the coolest water I could stand, because hot water sent my rash to the highest pinnacles of torture and itching. I laid out my makeup and wearily put on my advertising face, blew dry my advertising hair, stepped into my advertising clothes, made the bed, and went downstairs.

Though I was, and still am, a true believer in the sacred rite of eating dinner together as a family, breakfast was a pretty solitary affair at the Keiffer house. Not being morning people, Larry and John preferred to eat their cereal in silence, interrupted only by monosyllables and finger-pointing to indicate pass-the-milk, or pass-the-sports-page-please. As the two of them had to leave the house before I did, I ate my breakfast in silence, too, except when I opened the door to let the dog out and told her to "go be a good girl."

As usual, John and Larry had left the morning *Chronicle* scattered open all over the dining room table, but I wasn't in the mood to read about yesterday's murders or plane crashes. I sank down in a chair at the table. Almost too tired to hold my body upright, I propped my elbows on the newspaper and dropped my chin into my hands. *I'm probably getting smudges of newsprint on my jacket*, I thought. But I was too tired to care.

Come on, Ann, I nagged myself, *you've got to eat some breakfast; it's the most important meal of the day.* I forced myself to swallow one bite of the single slice of buttered toast I'd put on my plate. But it tasted like sawdust in my mouth, and my stomach lurched warily.

Okay, forget breakfast, I thought. *But get something done in the extra time before you leave the house. Throw in a load of laundry or unload the dishwasher. You're wasting time sitting here.* Though it was only 8:00 a.m., the morning already felt all used up. And so did I. I sat there for a few minutes, stale, tired, trying not to scratch, sipping hot tea from a chipped crockery mug.

As exhausted as I was, I couldn't let myself relax. I forced myself to get up from the table and tend to the laundry and the dishwasher. I was trying to hold myself together with inattention and the promise that soon some smart doctor was going to tell me how to cure my damnable rash. Then, I was sure, I'd feel better.

———

At that time, our family health insurance coverage was with Spectrum Health, a huge health maintenance organization (HMO) with offices throughout the San Francisco Bay area. I didn't have far to go to see a doctor about my rash that day in February. We lived just fifteen minutes north of the nearest Spectrum medical complex, an enormous facility that included a hospital and a large number of crowded clinics sprawling over two suburban blocks.

In a futile attempt to overcome its reputation for impersonal medicine, the Spectrum organization ran endless advertising campaigns urging its members to "choose a personal physician." But that was not an easy task. There were, after all, hundreds of doctors working for Spectrum. To me, there seemed no practical way to winnow down all those M.D.s to find the one right for me. I, like most Spectrum members, was resigned to playing Doctor Roulette. In spite of the "personal physician" propaganda, most of us still took the first available doctor — the Unknown Physician — because we all knew we got an appointment faster that way.

While I didn't have complete faith in Spectrum's dedication to my health and well-being, I felt the doctors there could surely help me get rid of a not-so-simple rash. In a haze of exhaustion, I drove to Spectrum, found my way to the right clinic, and slumped into one of the molded plastic waiting room chairs. With no desire to read the tattered year-old magazines littering the chipped formica tables, I simply sat there feeling tired, waiting for my name to be called.

Finally the nurse called my name, and I was parked in a cubicle for another twenty-minute wait. Then there was a cursory knock on the door, and my luck-of-the-draw for that day walked in. He was a lanky, gray-haired stranger with a smile so quick I didn't know whether to be warmed or warned by his sincerity.

Not wishing to be a whiner and wanting this doctor to like me enough to care about what was happening to me, I smiled back and then began to tell my story in detail. I held out my hands, showed him my elbows, knees, and feet. I told him about the terrible itching, the detective work I'd already done trying to track down any chemicals or foods that might be causing the problem. Then, all pretense of happy face gone, I looked to him for answers.

The doctor took hold of my hands, examined the raw, red bumps for several seconds, and then gave his diagnosis: "Well, I'd say you have a very nasty rash."

I knew that. My husband could have told me that. My thirteen-year-old son could have told me that. Without even looking up from what he was writing in my chart, the doctor off-handedly recommended calamine, low potency cortisone, or anti-itch gel from the drugstore.

Tears pooled in my eyes. Hadn't he understood? I told him I'd already tried all those things. Wasn't there something else I could do? I was so very tired. And I wasn't sleeping well. Was there some chance this rash and my sleep problems could be caused by stress?

Momentarily interested, this doctor looked up. "What kind of work do you do?" he asked. I told him I worked in an advertising agency in San Francisco. Without a pause he adopted a wink-wink-nudge-nudge attitude, and with a conspiratorial smile asked if maybe I'd been messing around with some recreational drugs up in the city.

I couldn't believe what he was saying. I looked over at him and spoke with all the conviction my worn-out body had in it. "No. Absolutely not," I declared.

With that, my hope began to wither. It was obvious this doctor had no miracles tucked away among his sheaves of carbonless lab slips and prescription blanks. If he didn't know what was wrong with me, would anyone else? I hated to think what it was going to be like to live forever with the devil's own affliction. Tears of exhaustion and frustration rose up to ride the rims of my eyes. Desperate for some reason I felt so lousy, I asked him, "Do you think I should see a psychiatrist or something?"

"Don't worry about it," he said. "You're just a little high strung. Why don't you try to relax?"

"Here," he said, handing me a prescription form, "take these when you can't get to sleep. Come back and see me if you need to . . . and just try to relax."

Try to relax. Oh, Lord. Now I was even more unstrung at the thought of sleeping pills, this Halcion, whatever it was, written on the prescription form I held in my hand. All I could think of was my father, his illness, his depression, and the careless doctors who put the monkey of medical addiction on his back. No, I surely didn't trust doctors. Or their medications.

Besides, sleep wasn't my only problem. What was I going to do about this itching disease? I just didn't think I had what it took to deal with it day after day for the rest of my life.

As I sat there in the examining room that morning, I wanted to put my head down and weep. But it seemed if I ever let myself start to cry from the depth into which I was falling, the tears might never stop.

Something was definitely wrong with me, but I had to knit up my raveled nerve ends and leave, solution or no solution. I walked over to the sink, ran cold water on some industrial-strength paper towels, and held their coolness on my rash. I simply couldn't let myself cry now. I decided I'd better get this prescription filled just in case.

Then I had to get to work.

———

I've heard that, in the language of the Eskimos, there are a multitude of words for snow because snow is so intimately known to the Eskimo people and so intricately woven into their way of life. By late spring of 1983, I needed a multitude of words for exhaustion.

I was wearing down, cell by cell, grinding, grinding down. Though I was aware of my fatigue as a garment of lead I wore every day, I did not comprehend the full extent of what was happening to me. It was rather like how we, as parents, can't see how fast our children are growing until we're away from them for a few days. We're simply too close to see the changes because the changes are taking place so gradually, but so inexorably, day by day.

I'm sure if you'd asked me, I would have vowed that Larry and John were the number one priority in my life, and work was number two. But the way I spent my energy probably proved otherwise. As for my own well-being, it didn't merit a place on my priority list at all. Though I did not understand it at the time, my Duke-self was in charge, and he was refusing to have his goals thwarted by a sick woman. He despised my weakness, despised me for my illness. I had so thoroughly abdicated to Duke that Valentine and I were now being ground to dust under the heel of my masculine values.

Had I been able to continue at the rate I was going, I could have qualified for the Associated Press Most Valuable Player on an Advertising Team Award that year. It wasn't the hours I worked; it was the *way* I worked — nonstop, at a pace akin to a full-court press in basketball. I drove myself to achieve, do, reach the next goal, finish the next assignment. I thought I was what I produced.

On my agency time sheets almost all of my hours were billable to a client — meaning no downtime, no professional reading, no chit-chat, and no common sense. I ate lunch at my desk. As soon as I ripped one assignment out of my typewriter, I rolled in a new piece of paper to begin the next. The more advertising I wrote, the more successful the presentations I made, the more awards I won, the harder I worked, the more I strived to achieve. I thought I *was* my job. And I was still trying to prove I was a good worker.

On top of that, as any working mother knows, when my day at the office was done, my work at home was only beginning. At 5:30 or 6:00 p.m. every day, I hurried to my car and clenched up to drive home with hundreds of thousands of other Bay Area commuters in the stop-and-go, bumper-to-bumper freeway traffic. I drove only thirty-five miles an hour, but I was still going fast — pumping adrenalin, my mind careening back and forth between some creative problem I was working on at the office, what in the world I was going to fix for dinner when I got home, or how close I was coming to the guy's bumper up ahead.

Larry had begun pitching in on household duties soon after I'd started my job, and I only had one son to worry about. So I wasn't a drudge at home. It's just that I didn't know how to turn off my stressful ways, my goal orientation, my slavery to tasks. I was driven at home as well as at the office, always seeing the next shirt to be ironed, the next bed to be made, the next toilet bowl with a brackish ring, the next problem I thought I should tackle to help John along on his path through life.

I can remember times in the late spring of that year when I arrived home thinking I could not stand to hear the sound of another human voice. My nerves were so shot, any noise felt like a physical assault. Sometimes, in desperation, I'd shut myself in the bathroom just to avoid having to hear the cartoon noises coming from the TV or the telephone or John's karate kicks and mouth-made sound effects ricocheting off the furniture and the walls. But somebody had to start dinner, and that somebody was me. So I'd tie on my apron and go to work to beat the dinner-hour clock in the kitchen.

I remember one night in June when I looked down in consternation to see my hand shaking so badly that a thin splatter of spaghetti sauce was traced across the front of my apron and on the stove. I put down the wooden spoon as if it were at fault, tried to tell myself I was just a little more rushed than usual. And I almost believed it.

During the one time I'd always counted on for communion — our family dinner hour — I still couldn't unwind. My mind ran and leaped like a rat trapped in a metal cage wired for electric shocks. In a frantic attempt to be upbeat, I race-talked my way through my advertising day, my tongue tearing over my words as if they were speedbumps. I talked so fast I could barely understand myself. Though I felt this urgent need to be supportive of Larry, when he'd launch into sharing the play-by-replay of his nightly racquetball game, my mind was too distracted to listen. Though I felt the same kind of urgency about mothering John, my efforts amounted only to policing his homework and checking his face to see if he looked happy. Which he did not.

I was winding, winding tighter and tighter; my mainspring was wearing out. Often, after a day at the office, I'd tell Larry I felt as if the blood had been sucked out of my face. At night, I could barely climb the stairs to go to bed;

my legs felt like two-hundred-pound appendages of wet sand I had to drag up one step at a time. Grab the banister, lift leg, pull, step, repeat. It seemed to take forever to make the journey up those two short flights of stairs some nights. And when I reached my bed, there was no relief.

My sleep grew more and more erratic. Out of desperation and with great uneasiness, I tried the prescription for Halcion the doctor at Spectrum had given me. But I soon decided the pills were less than worthless. Maybe they did help me go to sleep, but it wasn't a restful sleep. Within two hours I'd rebound wide awake — the way a rubber ball bounds to the surface after you hold it under the water — feeling jangled, and more anxious and desperate than before.

Even on those few nights when I did fall asleep for a few minutes or a few hours, I woke groggy and tired with a kind of gray heaviness that filled every cell of my body. Sometimes I'd lie awake crying from exhaustion and frustration, not knowing why someone who was so tired could not do the one thing she needed most: sleep.

At the same time my weight began to drop. I wasn't trying to lose weight; I just couldn't eat much of anything. I felt too wrung out, sick, and exhausted to eat. At first, I got some perverse pleasure out of being able to button my skirts and twirl them around my disappearing waist, hips, and thighs unhindered. And if my slacks were sliding off my hips, gee, that was kind of a novelty for a lady who'd always had a more than ample bottom. But something definitely wasn't right.

As time went on, the chills hit. Not every day, but often, waves of icy cold would prickle up and down my body. I'd go to bed wearing two nightgowns, my robe and socks, covered by all the spare blankets in the house. Still I could not get warm. Eventually, sometime during the night, I'd drench myself in sweat. But I never had a fever.

As for the rash, after two more appointments and as many dead ends, a Spectrum dermatologist tentatively diagnosed my rash as dermatitis herpitaformis — an inability to tolerate gluten found in wheat, oats, rye, and barley. But the drug treatment of choice did not seem to work for me. My rash raged on unchecked.

———

It may seem that even though I did not comprehend the extent of my decline, other people would have noticed what was happening to me and warned me. But my family was back in Ohio, and I hadn't seen any of them in more than two years. Even my closest friends rarely saw me. I was too busy to go to lunch during the week and, by the end of the week, I was too tired to socialize or put on my hostess face for anyone.

One morning, one of my co-workers at L&B looked up with concern as he watched me come in the door at the agency, and said, "Ann, are you all right? You haven't seemed like yourself — you know, bubbly — in a long time." I said I guessed I was just tired.

But later, while I was washing out my coffee mug in the restroom, I looked at my face in the mirror. It was strangely puffy and pasty pale with heavy blue circles under the eyes. I'd seen better-looking things lying face up in the satin-lined confines of caskets.

Larry was the one who expressed the greatest concern about me. Though I tried to be upbeat, he could see my body was giving out. He was worried about what I was doing to myself and asked if I couldn't ease up a little at work. But he didn't insist that I do something to alter my crazed ways; he trusted my judgment. Looking back, he now regrets that very much.

Realistically, I know there was no way Larry could have prevented what was about to happen. I was incapable of listening to even Larry's most impassioned pleas to stop what I was doing. I had no desire to listen to reason, because I had what I wanted: my job at L&B. I was not going to be a wimp who couldn't make it in the fast lane of prestigious, big-time advertising. I was not going to give in to my fatigue and illness. All of my colleagues could handle the pace, and I would, too.

The rest of that spring I willfully ignored my body. By June, however, I was so sick and precarious, I went to Victoria and asked if I could move my week of vacation up from August to early July. Victoria said that wouldn't be possible because Jamie, one of the art directors, already had her vacation scheduled for that time. She said L&B couldn't get by with two members of its creative team gone at once — and I believed her. I turned to leave Victoria's office, but I so needed some time to take care of myself that I took one final shot at getting it. "What if I could get Jamie to switch weeks with me?" I asked.

"That would be fine," Victoria said, "No problem."

I went down the hall to Jamie's office immediately and asked if she would be willing to trade vacation weeks. Jamie said she was sorry, but she and her family had already booked and paid for a houseboat to cruise the Delta, and she couldn't get her money back at that late date.

I didn't bring up the subject of vacation again. After all, the L&B office really couldn't get along with two members of its creative team gone at once, now could it? I decided I'd simply have to hang in until August. I could make it until August, I thought.

But I didn't know then that the body never lies. All through June and July, as I pushed on and on, I got sicker and sicker. My rash raged. I lost twenty precious pounds, leaving me with hollow thighs, pencil wrists, and bird-bone arms. Still I struggled on, my armored-tank ego crashing toward the goal inside a body of spun glass.

Until the final crisis finally came over a bagel.

4

Breakdown
Over a
Bagel

*T*he day before "The Day of the Bagel" had been a big one at L&B. All of the honchos from the New York corporate offices were in town to review the creative work our office had been doing for West Coast clients — at least that was the pretext. Our visitors may have been using the review only as a good excuse to check into one of San Francisco's four-star hotels, dine out on their expense accounts, and gather some hilarious California "flake" stories to take back to the Big Apple.

At any rate, all of us in the San Francisco offices of L&B had been preening for this pitch for weeks. Impressing our corporate mucky-mucks was almost as important as winning a new client. So we were prepared to trot out every dog and pony we owned and put on a show that would leave them all sucking their teeth.

My presentation boards were ready and waiting in the office. I thought of them anxiously as I got out of bed that morning. I was gray-green with exhaustion and wired to quivering with the hype of the day ahead. After I'd dragged myself ready, I drank some Pepto Bismol straight from the bottle to try to settle my stomach. I was afraid I wouldn't be able to get from home to the office without emptying my belly somewhere along Highway 101.

Before the big presentation I put a cup of ice on the conference table — for use in keeping my rash under control. I was most of the way through a pack of Rolaids and sick all over with a desperate fatigue by the time it was my turn to present. But when I got the floor, I was brilliant.

I was responsible for showing the creative work we'd produced for a major auto insurance company. Now if that sounds dull to you, it's because you weren't there. My ills belonged to someone else for the few minutes I was presenting. I tap danced my way through those presentation boards with all the joy and glee working in advertising had ever given me. I was dramatic. I was funny. I had the New Yorkers and my own cohorts loving that insurance story and laughing out loud. I was in my glory — and sicker than I'd ever been in my life. Not a soul in the room knew but me.

———

When my alarm rang the following morning, I was so profoundly fatigued I felt as if I'd been given an elephant sedative. Resolutely, I hauled myself up to a sitting position on the side of the bed, got my feet on the floor, then had to push against the mattress with both hands to shove myself up and out of bed.

I went into the bathroom and stood in the shower for a few minutes longer than it took to wash my hair and rinse off, hoping the water would somehow rejuvenate me for the workday ahead. Blow-drying my hair, putting on my makeup, getting dressed — every movement in my routine was a struggle, as if I were moving under fathoms of murky, weighty water. I was drawn out, stretched thin, brutalized by fatigue. But it did not occur to me to stay home.

Strained, ill, and exhausted, I drove to San Francisco and parked my car in the parking garage across from L&B. As was my usual routine, I walked four blocks to Barclay's, a deli L&Bers frequented so often for take-out-to-eat-at-your-desk food we knew the entire menu by heart.

I got in line behind ten other sleep-wrinkled people inching along in front of the glassed-in serving counters displaying muffins, fresh fruit, and warming bins of french toast, bacon, sausage, and scrambled eggs. But all I wanted was my daily bagel.

When I reached the cashier, I asked for a raisin cinnamon bagel, plain, no butter, no cream cheese. With the deft motions of someone who's performed a chore hundreds of times, the cashier slipped my bagel into a little waxed paper sack, handed it to me over the counter, and rang up the sale. "That'll be fifty-five cents," he said.

I looked down at the handful of coins I had shaken from my wallet just seconds earlier. There, in that instant, my life broke into two ragged pieces. Before and the Unthinkable After.

I did not know anything about those coins. Not their names. Not their values. Nothing.

I stared at the coins without recognizing them, saw them as if from a very great distance. Something in my head had shut down. An iron wall of confusion had dropped between me and the outside world.

> *Something I don't know. No-thought. Something I don't know. No-thought. What is it I'm trying to think of out there? No-thought. Something I should know. Don't know. Fear. Extreme fear. Don't know. No-thought.*

Up until that moment I believed I owned my brain, that it was at my command. But I had suddenly become its prisoner, a powerless victim of some malfunction in my own brain.

> *No way out. Don't know. What is it I don't know? No-thought. No-thought. Struggle for thought. No-thought. Terror. Whirling, whirling void of no-thought. Don't know. Don't know. No-thought.*

I have no idea how long my brain was actually shut down. Probably only seconds, though it seemed like hours. Before the cashier could realize I was in trouble, basic information about coins slowly began to come back to me.

> *Thought. Money. Coins. Names of coins. Names. Yes, names.*

After several vigilant seconds, I could finally name what I saw in my hand: dimes, nickels, quarters, pennies. Ten cents, five cents, twenty-five cents, one penny.

Carefully, methodically, shakily I paid the man his fifty-five cents.

———

To prevent my muscles from twitching out of control in response to the adrenalin of terror, I clutched my arms and the bagel against my belly and started to walk the four blocks to my office. What-oh-what-oh-what-oh-what-in-the-name-of-God was happening to me?

My heart pounded so hard it echoed in my ears. Fear pricked my armpits and sent panicked spasms of heat and chills through my upper body. I was terrified my brain was going to short out at any moment and leave me stranded in that void again. Something dreadful was happening to me. Was I going insane on this ordinary day in June?

I struggled to throw nets over my fear as I walked straight through the brass-trimmed double doors at L&B and directly into Victoria's bright, sunny office.

Victoria was in early, sitting at her helter-skelter littered desk, working on a new business presentation. With terror shooting up and down my spine and quivering in my limbs, I skipped any pretense of morning pleasantries and said, "Victoria, I have to have downtime today. I can't write anything at all."

Never in my history at L&B had I made such a request. Evidently Victoria realized this was not the time to question me, because she only looked a little quizzical, then simply nodded and said okay.

I walked toward the safety of my office with my muscles twitching erratically and my heart pounding to get out of my chest. Just get to your office. Just get to your office. That's what I told myself. Once there, I rushed inside, shut my door immediately, and sank into the chair behind my desk.

I was coming unglued, stricken with the horrifying

possibility that my mind might shut down again. I hoped to God no one would need to talk to me or see me that day. Maybe, if I could just be alone and have time to pull myself together, I'd be all right.

From my in basket I pulled the latest copy of *Adweek* magazine and opened it on my desk, pretending to read while my mind raced on, frantically trying to figure out what I should do. Should I call Larry or my friend Dulcie . . . let someone know what had just happened? What if I couldn't even drive home?

Just then there was a shave-and-a-haircut knock on my door. There was no way of hiding out at L&B, because the architect had designed each office with a huge window onto the hall. Franklin stuck his head around the corner and looked in through my window at me, pantomiming, "Can I come in?" What was I going to do, pantomime back, "No, I'm busy losing my mind in here"? So I reluctantly nodded yes.

Franklin swung the door open, looking all starched and GQ, and grabbed a seat in the chair in front of my desk. He was holding a piece of paper. "'Morning, beautiful," he said, "Victoria told me you're taking some downtime today. So I thought maybe you could give me some feedback on this letter I want to send out today."

The mere fact that he was in my office showed me Victoria had not guessed the true state I was in, so that was good news. But I was frantic with the need to be alone. The most expedient thing to do was to tell Franklin yes, so he'd leave. That's what I did. Franklin flashed his smile and said he really appreciated it as he handed me the letter. Then he left, closing the door behind him.

By now I was whirling infinitely fast on a stiletto point

of fear. Maybe if I made myself get down to business-as-usual for a few minutes, I told myself, I'd feel better. But when I tried to read the letter, my brain shorted out again.

This time I could not read. Could not focus my thoughts. I had lost all ability to concentrate. I could not comprehend what was written on the page. Franklin's direct, well-structured sentences were lying there completely unintelligible to me.

No, I could not, would not let whatever this was happen. I pushed and shoved at my mind, *making* it read that page. With enormous effort I was finally able to comprehend what was written there on the L&B letterhead. But when I picked up my red pen to write my comments in the margin, I found another system breaking down. I could barely write. My coordination was erratic. The red felt-tip pen made jiggly, wiggly letters that looked exactly like every nerve in my body felt.

Somehow, by will alone, I urged and flogged my strung-out mind until it functioned just well enough for me to make the necessary comments on Franklin's letter. I don't remember returning it to him. I don't remember how I got through the rest of the day. I don't remember driving home. I know only that there were even worse days — and nights — to come.

———

School had just let out for the summer, and by grace alone it had already been arranged that John was staying with a friend during those first two weeks of vacation. Maybe it would have been better if he could have lived in someone else's happy home for the next year. But at least he wasn't at home those next two weeks, watching while his mother fell apart in a million burned out, used up pieces.

I cried nearly all night after I got home from L&B. Don't imagine a grown woman sniffling quietly and wanly into a Kleenex. Picture the most exhausted little child you've seen in your entire life. Picture a sobbing, wailing toddler so tired and so worn out you have to undress that inconsolable little person and put her to bed — a little kid sweating with the added fatigue of crying, and streaming enough tears and snot to fill twenty Kleenex.

I remember when John was a preschooler and got what I called "over-the-edge" tired like that. After I'd wrestled him into his pajamas while he thrashed and cried, I'd try to rock him and rub his back to help him quiet down, so he could go to sleep. But it hardly ever worked. Usually, he'd keep on sobbing and thrashing until exhaustion alone finally slipped him over the brink into sleep.

I was almost thirty-eight years old, and that's the way I cried. Except for one thing. I was too jangled and wrecked to slide over the brink into the healing depths of sleep.

During the early part of that long evening, Larry sat on the edge of the bed and tried to talk to me and calm me with an engineer's logic. No matter what had happened, I was home. I was safe. I was going to be okay. But there were no more logic circuits left in my brain.

Finally, Larry gave up and just held me while I sobbed. He undressed me and put me to bed, and still I cried. I couldn't understand what was going on. I loved my husband. I had a terrific son. I had a great job. What was the matter with me?

One last thing Larry told me as he got into bed with me to hold me tight: I was not going to work the next day. No matter what.

———

Before Larry left for work the next morning, he looked at my haggard face and asked if I wanted him to call L&B for me. But I told him no, I could handle it. He left, then, reminding me to rest and to call him at work if I needed anything.

I dreaded making that phone call, but I was not going to take the easy way out and let Larry do it. I sat tensely by the phone, waiting until I knew Victoria would be in her office at L&B, rehearsing my I-just-need-a-short-vacation speech. I was determined to maintain my image as her upbeat, supportive, hard-working copywriter who just needed a little rest. After all, that was what I desperately wanted to believe myself.

But when my call went through the switchboard and I got Victoria on the line, in spite of all my resolve, I broke down crying. There I was sobbing my guts out right in the ear of my self-controlled boss. Victoria, who never let her darker emotions run around naked or messy in public.

Used up, tasting shame like alum in my mouth, between sobs I said what Victoria had probably already guessed, "This is Ann . . . I can't come in . . . I'm sorry . . . I'm really sick . . . sorry . . . I have to take some time off."

There was a long pause, during which I continued to cry and apologize, and Victoria, I'm sure, was deciding how best to handle her over-the-brink copywriter. Finally, out of duty to the agency, she asked gently, "How much time do you think you'll need?" I said maybe a week or two. And we agreed optimistically to leave it at that.

———

As I hung up the phone, I could picture Victoria going

into Franklin's office to tell him what had happened. Could picture her going around to the entire staff individually to tell them that Ann was going to be out sick for awhile. I could imagine their questions, but not Victoria's answers.

Life would go on at L&B without me. As for me, I could not go on. I laid my head down on the carpet, and I wept.

I wept for myself, for my rash that would not go away, for my illness, for my job, for my exhaustion, for not eating or sleeping, for Larry who had to put up with my instability and my tears, for John who had a mother who was screwed up, for doctors who had no answers for me. And for whatever fatal inner flaw I had that was beginning to take away my life.

5

A One-Way
Ticket
Off the Planet

So began the fall that would take me to the bottom.

For the next two weeks, with effort, I existed. I was so worn out I felt hollow, empty of everything except despair. I left the house only to walk. Even though my feet were oddly stumbly and out of sync with my brain, it was still somehow comforting to set them down heel-toe, heel-toe on miles and miles of sidewalk.

The only part I dreaded about walking was what followed: I always had to come back home to be alone with me.

Alone, I had no distraction from my raging rash, my gray-sick fatigue, and the fear that I was going insane. I was too brain-scrambled to concentrate or read. Too ill to cook or eat. Too tired to accomplish much more each day than to make the bed and empty the dishwasher.

Worst of all, when I was alone, I was plagued by terrible remembering — by images of my father so many years ago, tipped back in his recliner chair. I saw him sitting there in the dark of my memory, unspeaking, withering, dying out his days in a depression that never lifted. Like father, like daughter? The thought affected me like hands tightening on my throat at 2:00 a.m.

For each of those fourteen nights, I lay in bed thin and frail, feeling more and more certain now that a person could die of sleep starvation. Clenched with fear and fatigue, I kept my face turned away from the clock, not wanting to see it flick off the passing seconds, minutes, hours, each flick mocking my gut-thinned, silver-thread hunger for sleep.

On one desolate night, lying awake at 1:30 a.m., I remembered the accepted wisdom that depression is anger turned inward. So I tried to make myself be angry. I woke Larry and mocked up a rage at L&B, Victoria, Spectrum, my own body; Larry agreed I had reason to be mad. In the end, though, I knew it had all been a charade. Yes, I had stresses and disappointments, but none that pained me this much. Larry went back to sleep, but I could not.

On some of those nights I was so afraid of where my life was leading that I could not lie in the bed. Trembling, I'd go to the den to study a stress-reduction workbook I'd recently purchased. Where was I going wrong? Negative thought patterns? Probably. Poor coping skills? Surely. The pages of the workbook were often puckered with tears, but for all my searching I couldn't find a single answer.

On the nights I couldn't think well enough to use the workbook, I'd just sit there in the dark, staring at the stripes of moonlight streaming through the blinds, feeling desperate, crying, praying, raging at my girlhood God. Please do *something* to help me. Something. Anything.

On each of those disintegrating nights, Larry would get out of bed and come looking for me. Pinched by sleep and worry, he'd sit on the chrome-and-brown-leather footstool in front of his favorite chair, trying to talk me down from my exhausted, near-hysterical crying. "Why can't you just go to sleep?" he'd ask. "You need sleep. Don't you know that?"

How could I explain my ragged wakefulness to a man who plummets into deep sleep at the touch of a pillowcase? I couldn't even explain it to myself.

"I know I need sleep — don't you think I know that? But I've forgotten how. I don't know how to sleep. I just can't sleep anymore. And I'm so scared."

How could I explain to someone who hadn't lived it the terrible portent of my father, silent in his chair? My sorrow for my father, my guilty anger at what I had thought of as his weakness, my fear that now I might end up living the rest of my life in a depression just like his.

Each night Larry would come to me and talk until all his carefully constructed attempts at reason broke under the burden of my unreasonable tears. Tears that had no reason except I was tired, I was so tired. And so afraid.

What is wrong with me? I'd beg to know as we sat there together. But neither of us had an answer. I was turning into a crazy woman. I felt frayed and worn like a bad lamp cord — waiting helplessly for the moment my exposed electric nerve endings would burst into flame, causing serious and irreparable damage.

Always in the back of my mind I waited. Waited for the moment when Larry would turn away, reject me in anger, frustration, or disgust. He never did. He was frustrated, I know. Probably angry sometimes. Inconceivably, he kept on loving me. Loved me not for the way I used to be, but as I was right then — with my ravaged face and body, my sobbing, and my panic. Loved something so deep down in me that it could not be diminished by illness, age, or disappointment.

In the months ahead I would come to be astonished at the stabilizing gravity force of that love, indeed, its healing power. But I did not recognize the possibility of such a miracle yet. In those last days of July, I was wavering so far out on my tether, I knew only that having Larry's arms around me was the one good thing I had left.

I was falling, falling, falling into chaos.

———

Don't think I fell into the black abyss without a fight. For weeks I struggled to grab for any handhold that would keep me from plummeting all the way to the bottom. My closest friends — Dulcie, Lorna, and Cecile — with whom I'd shared so much over the years reached out to me in every small way they could. But I was going down with such weight and force they could not stop my fall. Their phone calls, all my affirmations and positive thinking, Larry's midnight vigils — nothing, absolutely nothing, helped.

By the end of July, 1983, I viewed therapy as the last little spindly root protruding from the wall of the pit down which I was plunging, my last chance to grab onto something firmly planted and to hold tight. If the doctors at Spectrum couldn't find the cause of my rash or my crying and fatigue, then I *must* need psychiatric help. What was happening to me simply wasn't normal. So I called Spectrum and scheduled an appointment with the Unknown Therapist.

As with all other aspects of health care at Spectrum, psychiatric patients were assigned on a next-available basis, unless the patient knew a specific therapist to request. Since I didn't know anyone and was being rapidly sucked down into chaos, I took an appointment with the first therapist who could see me.

Limp and cool of handshake, tall, thin to the point of anorexia, a white lady's afro atop her tiny head, my new therapist, Sherrie, did not inspire confidence in me. She seemed tentative and uptight, less knowledgeable and confident than I was, and I was a sobbing basket case.

Still, I told myself, *looks can be deceiving.* So in those first fifty minutes, I poured out my whole messy story to Sherrie, spewing untidy colorfalls of words and emotions in Sherrie's beige room, filling Kleenex after Kleenex.

It seems impossible to me now, but in the midst of that cathartic telling, in between the tears, I joked. Yes, joked and even laughed. Perhaps I made light of what was happening to me because it was so unspeakably dark, perhaps because part of me was still healthy. Or maybe I was just trying to breathe air into the tiniest little bubble of hope. But somehow I found it in myself to laugh.

Sherrie sat at stiff attention in her beige chair and listened to this well-groomed, joking, articulate — if sobbing — Ann Keiffer and came to the conclusion her new patient was, yes, stressed, but basically sound. I later learned Sherrie wrote this assessment in my chart after our first session: "Ann Keiffer — stress reaction, prognosis excellent, patient very motivated."

Very motivated, indeed. In my relentless attempt to be upbeat and positive, I'd shot myself in the foot — or rather, the psyche. I walked out of the Spectrum Department of Psychiatry teetering on my high heels, wobbly with emotion and exhaustion, but Sherrie did not have a clue I was in danger. My light still worked. She had not seen that the wires of the cord were now almost completely exposed.

———

Even though I felt I hadn't connected with Sherrie, I made myself go back to see her the following week. But I left that second session more distressed and discouraged than ever because, for all my crying and talking, I was not starting to feel even the tiniest bit better.

In between those two sessions with Sherrie, I'd met with Dr. Wong, one of the prescribing psychiatrists at Spectrum, and he sent me away with a prescription for tranquilizers. I anguished over taking even one of the capsules. I was afraid — my father, oh, my father. Codeine, Demerol, Thorazine, Stelazine, all to feed that secret monkey on his back. And his depression never went away. Even when I occasionally and reluctantly gave in and took a tranquilizer, I still slept only in brief, anxious knots. I did not feel better. And I cried and cried and cried.

How was I ever going to get ready to go back to work? My agreed-upon one week of vacation was long gone, and my six weeks of sick leave were going fast. Although Victoria had not called to push for a firm date on which I'd return to work, Franklin began to call frequently to check on my status. I was in no shape to talk to anyone, so Larry acted as my go-between. According to Larry, Franklin was as solicitous as Florence Nightingale over the phone. According to Victoria at a much later date, Franklin was more like Nurse Ratched, demanding that Victoria either fire me and get my butt off the payroll, or get me back in the office. All I knew was that time was running out.

Time had already run out for me as a mom. When John came home from his trip, I tried to keep my distress hidden from him. I was aching with guilt, not wanting John to worry about me. But body language was John's mother tongue. He read every tense muscle, every line in my face, every withheld tear, every unsaid agony. He knew.

At the precarious age of thirteen, what can a young man do when his mom is breaking down right in the next room? Very little. So John withdrew — retreated to his room, talked on the phone with friends for hours, watched TV, and kept his feelings locked inside. Even so, his loving sadness leaked out through the light in his eyes. I knew he knew. All my attempts to reassure him I was going to be okay were whispers thrown against a raging wind.

I think Larry believed that, any day now, I'd snap out of this depression and have some kind of spontaneous recovery. Nevertheless, he was concerned. So, in an attempt to help me pull out of my agony, he suggested we celebrate our anniversary a week early and go to Lake Tahoe. There I'd have nothing to do but eat out, sleep in, and get well, he said. I was willing to try anything. So we packed our bags and left for what we hoped would be a relaxing getaway.

We couldn't have been more uncomprehending of reality if we'd both been in comas. We were so desperately naive.

———

Determined to make this a miracle vacation, Larry and I splurged on a beautiful room at a new motel close to the blue-green waters of Lake Tahoe's rocky shore. Decorated in contemporary tones of peach and soft teal, with white-washed woods, our room was as restful and lovely as a room could be. From way inside myself, I looked at that room with longing for the-way-things-used-to-be. I wanted to appreciate it — could appreciate it, a little, but only from a very great distance. Only from the memory of what I *once* would have loved before I'd gone so dead inside.

Larry unpacked and swiftly settled into his vacation routine — read, sleep, run, sun, sleep, read, sleep. I swiftly drifted into deep water.

Every bite of food I brought to my mouth was swallowed under protest. I tried to read but couldn't focus my attention on the paperback I'd brought along to pass the time. I felt used up, reamed out, too brain-tired to read. I did walk every day, always wearing sunglasses so no one could see my swollen eyes and ruined makeup. But I knew I wasn't going anywhere. I felt separate, alien, and utterly hopeless.

On our second night at the lake, Larry and I got dressed up and went out, determined to have a festive anniversary dinner. I wanted so much to be the happy anniversary celebrant, but it was all a lie. I wobbled to our table on shaky legs, tried to smile, make conversation, feel a spark of love and happiness. But all I felt was dead. Completely and absolutely dead.

Though I'm embarrassed to tell you this, I must, so you will know the depth of my fear. I spent every night of our stay in Tahoe sitting on the white tile floor of our beautiful bathroom, leaning my head on the toilet seat, gagging. Gagging just the way I did when I was six years old and so very scared to go to school. Not vomiting, just retching with fear until my throat was sore and my stomach muscles ached, desperately ill down to the very fiber of my being. And sleeping almost not at all for six straight nights.

I wasn't getting better; I was getting worse. Fear and exhaustion hung on me like a sodden canvas shroud. Worms of sadness ate the last living bits of my heart. *No more, no more, no more,* I thought. *I cannot live like this. I cannot live another minute this way.*

So, on August fifteenth, in a roiling anarchy of emotion, I clung to Larry. With tears streaming, my face buried in his shirt, my voice muffled and constricted, I finally said out loud the thought that had begun to consume me day and night. Five lethal words: I want to kill myself.

"I want to kill myself. I can't stand this anymore. I'm so sick. And why? Nobody knows why. There's no reason. I can't go on, not sleeping. All I want is a one-way ticket off the planet. All I want is to die."

I remember how Larry stood there, quiet, levelheaded, and disbelieving. At first. But after fifteen minutes, he hurriedly loaded me and all of our suitcases in the car. During our four hour drive home, I spent most of my time crying, wishing out loud to be dead, weeping my complete and utter fatigue and hopelessness.

"Ann, you don't want to die," Larry would say over and over, hoping to convince both of us, trying hard to remain calm.

My voice rising, my tears falling, I'd wail, "Yes! I do. I can't stand this any more. I'm sick. I'm crazy. Something is wrong with me. I can't live like this any more. I'm going to take all those stupid, worthless tranquilizers and get this over with."

Now, looking back, I think I didn't mean what I was saying — exactly. I think I was really saying, "Larry, this is how bad it is; please, please help me." But by the time we got home, neither of us was sure what I was capable of.

Without unpacking the car, Larry helped me upstairs and made me dial the therapist on call at Spectrum. I was sobbing so out-of-control it took several minutes for me to tell this person what was happening. Naturally, the on-call therapist didn't have my chart or know anything about me. He asked if I'd been given any tranquilizers, and I told him yes and which ones. Take two and lie down, he said. Larry took the phone from me, talked briefly, then hung up.

So tired I could not fight or protest, I let Larry help me to the bedroom while I cried. He searched out the plastic vial of tranquilizers, shook out two capsules, and handed them to me with a glass of water. I took the pills still crying. Larry peeled off my clammy clothes and settled me in bed. Within minutes I was finally, finally, sleeping.

———

I had no idea how much time had elapsed when I awakened, groggy, to find Larry standing by the bedside gently shaking me.

"Dulcie's on the phone," he said. "I've been talking to her; now she wants to talk to you."

I was pretty foggy, but I fumbled around and finally took the phone he held out to me.

"Ann," I heard Dulcie say, "you may not like what I'm going to say, but Larry and I have decided: You are going to the hospital."

Her words snagged me from my warm drug haze like an ice-cold meat hook. "No, no, no, no, no," I cried. The loony bin, the nut-house, the drool ward. Shame rose up from me and stank like rotten chicken. I couldn't. Oh, please, please don't let this be me. Don't let this happen.

"Yes. You're going to the hospital, and you're going to have a baby," Dulcie went on in a calm Dulcie-knows-best voice. "And the baby you're going to have is you."

More no, no, no. More tears. More horrible visions of myself, my father, in a locked ward. But Larry stood there beside me, nodding his head firmly in agreement — yes.

"Ann, you *are* going to the hospital," Dulcie said without even the slightest question in her voice. And in my heart I knew she and Larry were right. I submitted with the very last of my spirit leaking out in more despairing weeping.

"Put Larry back on the phone now," Dulcie said gently. And I did. They talked while I cried. Then Larry handed the phone back to me again.

"Bernard is coming to drive you and Larry to the hospital," Dulcie said. "He'll be there in just a few minutes, so get a little bag packed to take with you. You're going to stay there. And you're going to be all right. I love you."

Larry hung up the phone for me, then called Spectrum to get instructions about where to bring me. Afterward, he put his arms around me. His breath smelled like chewing gum and normal life as he tried to comfort me with words of hope while I cried.

A short time later, Bernard arrived at our front door — Dulcie's new husband, a man we were only beginning to get to know, a wheeling-dealing Frenchman with an affinity for power, fast talk, and joyful arguments. Here he was on our doorstep on a mission of mercy for his new wife's broken-down old friend.

Larry went downstairs and let Bernard in. They both came upstairs, and Larry helped me into my clothes while Bernard gathered up my bag of hospital necessities. I was so weak and so unsteady from the two tranquilizers, the men had to drape my arms around their shoulders to lift-carry me down three flights of stairs and out to Bernard's car. I felt like luggage sitting between the two of them on the front seat. I mean, what do you say on your way to the loony bin?

———

Dr. Robbins, the Chief of Psychiatry at Spectrum, was to meet us at the emergency room. Bernard drove his car under the ambulance portico, and Larry helped me out of the car and through the shooshing, rapid-open automatic doors. Once inside, we registered at the emergency room desk and were ushered into a small cubicle containing a gurney, a sink, stackable chairs, a generous supply of tongue depressors, and blue plastic puke basins.

Dr. Robbins arrived within minutes. I was relieved by the very sight of her. She was first of all, and surprisingly, a woman, and a young one at that — with long red hair casually pulled back and a calming, good-humored manner.

Dr. Robbins leaned against the gurney which was against the wall across from me, looked at me carefully, and began to ask me questions, sometimes shifting her gaze to Larry to get his point of view, too. Once more a buoyant little bubble of hope lifted in me, and I saw Dr. Robbins smile when I managed to make a very small joke.

Dr. Robbins drew up a chair across from me and then sat down. "I think I can tell you right now what's wrong with you," she said. "I think you have an organic chemical imbalance. That means because of stress or some other factor, your brain is lacking the chemicals necessary for the proper functioning of its neurotransmitters."

Now we were getting some place. I had something specific, and it had a name: an organic chemical imbalance. I was on the edge of the molded plastic chair on which I sat, physically wrung out like an old gray dishrag, but never in my life more eager to hear what someone had to say.

Dr. Robbins didn't go into much more medical detail, but I had the sense I was in good hands. She said she didn't recognize my rash and scheduled me for a complete physical the following week. After writing a prescription for antidepressants, she looked at me and nodded, stood up as if to go, then stopped, tapping her stethoscope thoughtfully on the palm of her hand.

"About hospitalization . . ." she said, "the only Spectrum inpatient psychiatric facility is across the Bay, and it's full. So you've got to promise me you're not going to do anything to harm yourself, then you can go home. Can you promise that?"

Of course I could promise that. I had *hope*!

"One more thing: It will take some time for this medication to take effect," she warned me. "You probably won't see any improvement for seven to ten days, so don't get discouraged. You'll be all right. You're going to need some time to fully recover."

I was almost giddy with relief as she handed me my prescription. But I was also more than a little scared at *not* being put in the hospital.

While we waited for my prescription to be filled, I remember thinking, thank God, I still won't have to check those boxes on questionnaires that ask if you've ever been hospitalized for mental illness. I was dizzy both with relief and colossal fatigue.

The antidepressants at last in my possession — more precious than diamonds to me — we went to the parking lot, got into Bernard's Oldsmobile, and drove home. We'd just arrived and unlocked the front door when the phone rang. It was Dulcie, and when Larry told her I was not in the hospital, I could hear her reaction through the telephone receiver and clear out in the kitchen where I was washing down my first antidepressant with a glass of water. Dulcie was horrified Spectrum had let me go. She told Larry not to do anything until she called back.

Within half an hour, she did call back — with a plan. Dulcie had phoned Lorna and arranged for me to stay with her for a week. Lorna's husband was out of town on a business trip, and Lorna had said she'd be glad to have me come there for R&R. Dulcie ended our long evening by saying she'd be over in the morning to pick me up and drive me to Lorna's.

I went to bed and actually slept.

———

On August sixteenth I felt like a blown-out egg, a vulnerable shell of a person with nothing but a little dried-up goo left inside. To me, it was both remarkable and embarrassing that my husband and my friends seemed to think I was worth taking care of.

I was amazed at Larry's capacity to love me, his patience in helping me pack, his nothing's-changed-between-us good-bye kiss that morning. And he was family. But who were these women, my friends? What did we mean to each other that they were willing to take me in when I had nothing left to offer but an empty shell?

Dulcie — tall and elegant, with curving dark hair and a narrow aristocratic face — had been my close friend for more than seventeen years. Even during the most difficult periods of Dulcie's life — her moldering first marriage; her son's near-fatal accident; no income and on her own after the divorce — she always seemed to have a gift for knowing exactly what needed to be done. And, with the single-minded purpose of a drill press, she saw to it that it was done.

An interior designer by profession, if Dulcie decided to, she could create order and beauty in a junkyard over-night — and have the junkyard dog fetching flutes of champagne on a silver tray, or he'd darn well find himself standing in line down at Doggie Unemployment.

Believe me, if Dulcie said you were going to spend the week at Lorna's, you were going to spend the week at Lorna's.

———

Lorna, her husband, two sons, and their golden Lab lived across the Bay in a big old house on a suburban street that dead-ended abruptly in the country. Actually, Lorna's older son was in college in Washington state, and it was his room in which I'd be staying once Dulcie delivered me.

Although I trusted Dulcie and Lorna, my adopted sisters, to take me over and take me in, I was reproachful of my own need. I would have given anything to be able to shed the burden of my depression like a snake, wriggling away, leaving behind an old skin. I was ashamed by what I perceived as my weakness, ashamed that I needed my friends to take care of me this way.

By the time Dulcie and I arrived at Lorna's, I was physically exhausted and emotionally drained just from attempting to appear "normal." Before we could ring the bell, Lorna opened the door to greet us. Petite and cute, with Snow White's coloring, Lorna looked like a woman Walt Disney could have created, with a little added playful sexiness.

Standing with my two friends on Lorna's front doorstep that day, I felt like a little kid arriving for a sleepover — but homesick and dead tired ahead of time. Lorna hugged both Dulcie and me. Then Dulcie bid us a hurried got-to-get-back-to-work good-bye, and Lorna took me upstairs to put my things away in my borrowed bedroom.

During the school year, Lorna operated a thriving child care center, but she was an interior designer by avocation, one who didn't know the meaning of the word "finished." Each time I visited Lorna's, I was struck by two things. First, a walking-on-angle sense of disorder and impermanence. Second, the exciting possibility of something beautiful and new always hanging in the air, as thick as wallboard dust.

Lorna's favorite pastime was gleaning design ideas from magazines, which she marked for future reference by turning down the corners of the pages. She was easily inspired, so her house was almost always torn up, in the middle of some redecorating project or another — the kitchen cupboard doors removed and sitting on the floor in the dining room, wallpaper steamed off walls, a mammoth hole cut and awaiting french doors, and always painting and repainting.

My bedroom was in the midst of just such an inspired Lorna overhaul, but it couldn't have been more perfect. Made white-glove clean for me, in its unfinishedness the room was Zen-like — soft gray walls, white woodwork, stripped of all furniture except a folding sleeping mat on the wooden floor. For a moment I had the illusion that if I would light some incense, I'd achieve instant *satori*, spiritual enlightenment. But I would find out there was going to be nothing instant about my recovery. Nothing instant at all.

———

Lorna's house proved to be a well-chosen sanitarium for me that first week on antidepressants. I spent much of my time in a state of tearful suspended animation — just waiting for my medication to take hold. Though I still felt like a dead person, I appreciated Lorna's company and sank into her relaxed lifestyle with at least some small degree of relief.

Following Lorna's nonroutine, we ate whatever we wanted, whenever we wanted, not hemmed in by mealtimes. We spent whole afternoons quietly looking through her stacks of house magazines with turned-down pages. Together, we tried to do lazy stretching exercises on the floor, with me finishing up counting ". . . eighteen, nineteen, twenty," only to find Lorna still back at a leisurely ". . . nine." I couldn't seem to match her more naturally calm pace even when I tried.

But it was when I was feeling scared and hopeless that I appreciated Lorna most. Lorna is the adult child of alcoholic parents, one who's worked hard to free herself from the past. In trying to come to terms with both her childhood and her tumultuous marriage, Lorna had done a lot of reading, self-analysis, and soul-searching, so she was able to just be a friend to me while I cried. She never thought I was going crazy or treated me like a dim-witted child. She simply sat with me and accepted whatever I was feeling.

How long until these antidepressants would take effect? How long, Lord? How long?

———

By the end of my week at Lorna's, my rash was still rampant; I was still exhausted and buried in the blackest of blues. I was eating again, however, even if it was a purely mechanical process having almost nothing to do with taste or pleasure. I was also beginning to sleep a little better. I felt I could slog on from day to day if I could sleep most of the way through each night. The best I could say was, while the antidepressants weren't antidepressing me yet, I was at least minimally functional.

When Dulcie came back to pick me up on my last day at Lorna's, the two of them had arranged for me to have a massage. I know my friends thought they were giving me a treat but, strange as it may sound, I was too tired for a massage. Even that pampering cost me more in energy than I had in my body bank. I was relieved when Dulcie finally picked me up and took me home, where I went gratefully up the stairs to claim my own bed and pillow again.

Later that afternoon John came home from swimming, calling out "Mom?" as soon as he came in the door. Once upstairs, he hugged me awkwardly, as if I were made of glued-together eggshells, and then sat down beside me, trying to make conversation. I think we were both relieved when the phone rang, and he had an excuse to put aside his bedside manners and go talk to a friend.

That evening, when Larry came home, I heard the click of the metal feet on his briefcase as he set it down in the tiled entry hall. He called my name and came quickly upstairs, bringing me a questioning smile and an unquestioning hug. He acted like someone who's read the fine print on the contract and was happy to sign in blood anyway.

For Larry, neither how I looked nor how badly my life fell apart seemed to have a bearing on whether or not he was going to love me. Even when I couldn't love me, he did. Though my emotions were beaten flat and dead, I was dimly awed by the quality of that love. How could he love me like that? Larry was on his way to becoming my healer.

———

Later on that first night home, my friend Cecile arrived unannounced with her two sons, carrying her concern on her face and a buoyant bouquet of mylar get-well balloons above her head.

Cecile and I had met more than ten years before when our boys were in nursery school together. Dark, with a bronzy olive complexion and curly salt-and-pepper hair, Cecile was all natural and ninety-nine percent fat-free, weighing just over a hundred pounds. Possessed by enough passionate intensity for ten ordinary humans, she was a deeply earnest spiritual and psychological seeker — a fitness enthusiast, a reader of esoteric books, a meditator, an eschewer of routine medicine, an eater of vegies, a devotee of the truth no matter how painful. When Cecile looked you in the eyes and asked, "How are you?", it wasn't a greeting. She really wanted to know.

Now here Cecile was, standing in my bedroom, looking into my eyes and asking, "How are you?"

What was I going to tell her?

6

Slow
Crash of
Dreams

*C*ecile was of the avoid-drugs-and-take-responsibility-for-your-illness school of health. So when I told her about my diagnosis, I suspected she might be mistrustful of the antidepressants Dr. Robbins had prescribed. I was right.

As I lay on my bed, scraping up words to tell her what had happened, I could see Cecile was trying not to pass judgment on my antidepressants out loud. But her thoughts were in her eyes and held precariously unspoken behind her lips. I felt uncomfortable knowing she was questioning my one small hope, however silently. Worst of all, I knew telling my cautious friend Cecile was only practice.

The most difficult person in all the world to tell about my depression was my mother. In most situations I have trouble drawing a line between what should be public and what private, because almost nothing strikes me as private. (I will tell my life story to strangers, as you know from reading this book.) But this was one time I wasn't sure I should be relating every miserable detail of my experience.

It wasn't just that my mother would worry about me, or that she, like Cecile, would have misgivings about medication — though I knew she would. No, I knew telling my mother about my depression was bound to unearth all the dark-day memories of my father: his unreachable despair, the snare trap of prescription drugs, his misery, and always the ominous possibility of suicide, a family's slow death watch.

No, I am not faint-hearted about most things, but I could not call my mother to tell her how low I had fallen. However, she knew I was not well and, within a few days of my return from Lorna's, my mother called me. When I picked up the phone and heard my mother's voice that night, I dredged my mind for acceptable words. Though I'd had almost no practice at withholding facts or feelings from her, I tried. Still, what little I said was enough. The sound of my voice told my mother everything there was to know; it was dragging, weary, strained, and tight with tears.

In the most benign words I could think of, I gave my mother a sketchy account of my collapse, leaning heavily on the hope that had come with my diagnosis. But when I mentioned the antidepressants, even over thousands of miles of phone line I could hear the knife blade of anxiety slide into my mother's breath. Feigning casualness, she asked, "Oh? What's the name of the medication?"

I felt a hot flash of anger I did not articulate. I visualized Mom in the kitchen of her house in the woods in Ohio, writing down the name of the medication on a pad of paper she kept by the phone. Within minutes of hanging up, she would take it next door to my sister Molly, an R.N., to get the lowdown on my drugs. I hated being checked up on, but I also understood the ghosts of depressions past that were haunting my mother that night. So I told her, Asendin, even spelled it for her. I told her — and felt like the second sick and decaying growth on the family tree.

Mom fell silent then. I knew she was struggling with emotion — Dad, me, terrible memories, grief. And love. A mother's love is never done, not even when her child is thirty-eight years old. I didn't say anything because I knew why she was mute. She once told me that when her thoughts are confused and her emotions in turmoil, she feels like an overwrought old dog that has to get away, go hide under the porch, and just pant for awhile. I knew this was one of those times for her. So I just let her "pant," and I sat there with tears in my eyes.

"I'm going to be all right, Mom," I finally said into the silence, though I didn't know if I believed the words myself.

With an ache in her voice and great effort, Mom finally spoke, "Would you like to come back home for awhile? You could just lie out in the yard where it's quiet ..." She swallowed hard, "... look up at the big trees."

Now I felt the ache in my throat. Tears slipped in between my words, "Oh, Mom. Thanks. I know you love me. I love you, too. But I need to be here."

I did need to be here. I didn't want to be anywhere but here. For here I had my home, my doctors, my friends, and John. Most important of all, here I had Larry, who had already proven he wasn't going to worry that I was crazy, or treat me too gingerly, or demand I simply shape up. He believed in me, not in the memory of my poor, tortured, long-dead dad.

Early that evening, just as I was pulling back the blankets so I could crawl into bed, the phone rang again. It was another long-distance call from Ohio; this time it was my sister Molly's husband, Glenn. Evidently, my mother had already told my brothers and sisters the unsettling news from California. She'd probably spilled tears into a cup of coffee at Molly and Glenn's kitchen table only minutes before. Now here was Glenn, whom I knew only long distance, reaching out to help.

As soon as my mother left their house that night, Glenn had quietly retreated to the bedroom to call me. He wanted to offer me the most precious thing he could think of — his wife, my sister, the nurse. He hadn't discussed the trip with Molly yet because he wanted to know how I'd feel about it. But, if they could arrange it, would I like to have Molly fly to California and take care of me?

My chest filled with an aching anvil, my mind with fond pictures of my baby sister, Molly, thirty years old — her tenderness, her eloquent brown eyes, her unstinting acceptance, her loving hands. But she and I were separated by far more than the eight years between us and three thousand miles. I felt unworthy to have Molly come, embarrassed again by my raw and ugly need. Besides, I knew Molly and Glenn couldn't really afford the plane fare, and Molly had two little daughters in Ohio who needed her, too. With a shame-filled heart, I thanked Glenn, but told him, no, I just couldn't handle having Molly come to help like that. I lied a little. I said I didn't need her.

Ironically my brother-in-law, Glenn, whom I barely knew, was the only one in the whole family, other than my mother, who had the courage to call me. As for the rest, their concern had to go unspoken.

On one hand, my brothers and sisters probably didn't know how used up and shattered I was, because I didn't write or call; it was all I could do to share my fears with my mother. On the other hand, I suspect the real reason I didn't hear from them was that any discussion of depression gave my family the shakes. The pain of my father's depression had left its mark on all of us, like some blue-black, skull-and-crossbones tattoo. My brothers and sisters probably couldn't think of a single safe or comforting word to offer. But I was sure my name was on more than one church's prayer chain and almost certainly on my siblings' lips.

———

So I stayed at home, nursing my frailties in California. Each long day I plodded through as if on a death march. I was exhausted and dulled down in a way that could not be relieved by rest or good food. I had not one spark of energy with which to fuel a normal life. It was all I could do to get through each day and try to keep the hope alive that tomorrow might somehow be better.

Strangely, even as ragged and fatigued as I was, I was also gripped by restlessness and impatience. In the past I'd usually gotten fidgety waiting the few seconds it took for a traffic light to change. Now my whole life was stuck at a red light. My body was broken down, but my motor kept gunning and racing. My sick leave was almost gone. I was determined I was not going to give up my terrific job and go back to free-lancing. But what could I do to get myself and my life out of this stall and on the move again?

The first step had already been laid out for me. Following Dr. Robbins's instructions, I kept my appointment for a complete physical at Spectrum. The Unknown Physician assigned to perform this task gave the impression he didn't like living in the States. His face was dour, his skin taut on his bald bony skull, and his brittle conversation made up entirely of "say ahs" and terse questions about my medical history. The only time he came near me was to tap my knee with his rubber mallet and to peer clinically into my eyes, ears, nose, and throat. He had the bedside manner of a user-unfriendly android made of ice. As I cashed in my lab slips, peed in a cup, gave several vials of blood, and had X-rays, I only hoped what Ice Man, M.D., lacked in warmth he made up for in diagnostic brilliance.

A few days after my physical, I had to return to Spectrum for my next appointment with Sherrie. But before I saw her, I was to have a brief appointment with Dr. Wong, my prescribing psychiatrist, as a follow-up to the physical.

Dr. Wong's office looked like temporary quarters, as if he'd decided not to bother with knickknacks or paintings or personal touches because he wasn't planning to occupy the room long. His desk was positioned opposite the door and pushed up against the wall underneath windows placed too high to provide any view except treetops and sky. When you walked into Dr. Wong's office, his back faced you unless he turned around in his chair to greet you.

During my initial medication appointment, Dr. Wong's back had given me the feeling I wasn't so bad off, as if I were just a casual visitor who'd dropped by to say hello. The people whose charts were on his desk must be the ones with *big* problems, because those charts were obviously Dr. Wong's primary focus in the room.

I knocked, and Dr. Wong responded with an automatic, "Come in." When I opened the door, he looked over his shoulder at me, and said, "Hi, Ann, how are you? Take a seat." By the time I'd taken a chair, he'd squared some papers and pulled my chart — uh, oh — off the pile on his desk.

I was eager to give Dr. Wong all the information fifteen minutes of time would allow. He was my prescribing physician, but we hardly knew each other; we met for just fifteen minutes once a month to discuss my medication. My therapy was with Sherrie; my pills, only, from Dr. Wong. I always wondered if he knew what she knew. Or, for that matter, what I knew. I felt like a marionette whose strings were being operated by two puppeteers — God forbid they should miscommunicate and get something tangled.

"First, let's go over your lab work," Dr. Wong said. He leafed through the pink, blue, and yellow lab slips clipped in the front of my chart. "Everything looks fine. Looks like all we're dealing with is a chemical imbalance."

"But I still don't know what a chemical imbalance is," I said. "Do you have something I could take home to read?"

Dr. Wong thought a moment, then retrieved two pieces of paper from the file cabinet. Someone had taken apart a small booklet, arranged seven of its pages in jigsaw puzzle fashion on two eight-and-a-half by eleven sheets, then photocopied the whole thing, cutting off one or two sentences at the bottom of each page in the process.

I was grateful to finally have in my possession some hard facts that might explain my chemical imbalance. But I wondered why Spectrum didn't have a ready supply of professionally produced educational handouts on psychiatric problems to give to patients. In the main hospital building Spectrum maintained an extensive patient education library complete with brochures, videos, books, and a nurse. Maybe in psychiatry problems were too complicated or unexplainable to be summed up in handy little pamphlets.

Turning my chart to a blank page, Dr. Wong then began to ask me specific questions — about my sleep (sleep through the night, but feel exhausted all the time), appetite (fair, I am eating again), libido (nonexistent), general state of being (feel like I'm ninety years old and an elephant has fallen on me). Just answering his questions was making me feel drained and tired.

Afterward, when I walked back out to the waiting room, I was dismayed by how drawn and blurry-eyed I felt. The demands of this one trip to Spectrum were putting me into overload, and I felt my circuit breakers threatening to shut me down again. I slumped into a chair and decided to read the information Dr. Wong had given me while I waited to see Sherrie. Although the paper made me feel vaguely as if it had been written for a mentally slow five-year-old, it also contained the basic information I'd been seeking:

> We now understand that most depression is caused by a deficiency of one or two special chemicals that carry messages from one nerve ending to the next, across the little gap between them, like little messengers. They deliver the message to the next nerve, then jump back to the nerve they came from. When there are enough messengers to do the job, there's no trouble. But when there are not, whatever that nerve transmission is supposed to do, doesn't happen. When this deficiency occurs in a person's arms and legs or trunk of the body, various kinds of loss of motion or limitation of function can occur. When the deficiency of messengers occurs in the brain, the result is depression.
>
> We don't always know why these messengers, those special chemicals that carry nerve impulses, become deficient. However, we do have medicines that

correct the deficiency, either by keeping the little messengers from being further destroyed or by preventing them from being removed from the gap between nerves where they're supposed to do their work.

In other words, we now say that depression is caused by a chemical imbalance in the brain, and antidepressant medication helps return brain chemistry to normal.

Just then, the receptionist called my name. Sherrie was waiting outside her door for me, and we greeted each other with careful smiles; she had, of course, been notified about my emergency room visit.

All through our session that day, Sherrie kept asking me questions I thought I'd answered before, about my relationship with Larry and John, about my childhood and my parents. I knew she was fishing for some emotional *cause* for my depression, but I felt I'd already hauled all the fish of any significant size out of that particular pond.

Back in Pennsylvania I'd found a therapist and spent four productive sessions working on my gut-churning tendency to swallow anger. Later, I'd explored my sadness and my anger over my father's depression. I'd taken those issues and my overachiever syndrome along with me to several seminars over the years. Wasn't I done with all that yet?

Admittedly, over the past weeks I'd been haunted anew by my father's sorrows. Without question, my recent crash was forcing me to confront the price I might be paying for overachieving, working without respect for my own needs just to win success and the approval of others.

I wasn't denying that my depression was a sign I needed to make significant changes in my life. But maybe, just maybe, I *wasn't* being pursued by some horrible sadness or hurt or resentment unidentified or unexpressed, as

Sherrie seemed to suspect. Maybe what I'd puzzled over so often these last few months was the simple truth: I loved my husband, my son, my job, my life — and I was sick anyway. Hadn't the material in Dr. Wong's pamphlet confirmed it was possible for me to be depressed *without* having a deep emotional problem? If so, what could I do on a practical level to reconstruct my life?

While Sherrie seemed intent on finding the shark hidden in the water, I thought what I needed most were ideas on how to bail out my lifeboat so I could start living again. Her casting about for nonexistent leviathans seemed a waste of time to me. Was I going to have to spend months catching Sherrie up, filling her in on what I already knew before we could proceed?

Obviously, Sherrie and I just didn't click. Earlier, when I had asked Dr. Wong about the possibility of changing therapists, he told me Spectrum discouraged patients from "shopping around." I was too bone-crushingly weary, sad, and discouraged to be assertive about my needs. If I had raised a fuss, I'm sure I could have found someone at Spectrum I liked better, but my ability to fuss was long gone.

Fortunately, Sherrie finally did put away her bait and hooks and give up her fishing expedition that day. Taking a different tack, she suggested that perhaps I should think about setting new goals. Including my career, but not *just* my career: relationships, friends, health, vacations, all other aspects of my life.

At last, here was something constructive I could *do*! Hope for a future fluttered in my throat as faintly as butterfly wings. I told Sherrie I'd bring in my new list of goals to share with her the following week.

Momentarily buoyed by my assignment, I found the courage to ask Sherrie one final question before our session ended. It was something that had been bothering me since the night Larry had taken me to the emergency room.

"In the olden days, yesterday or the day before," I said, "would they have called an organic chemical imbalance a nervous breakdown?"

Sherrie looked away uneasily, as if unsure of the correct answer or, perhaps, what answer I wished to hear. Hesitating, she knit her eyebrows and gave her answer so it sounded more like a question, "Uh, yes? I think so."

Sherrie really bugged me.

And the thought that I'd had or was having a nervous breakdown disgusted me more than diving naked into a backed-up sewer. Well, I'd asked for it. Now I knew. I was repulsed by myself — down to the very tiniest hidey-hole of my being. A nervous breakdown. Disgusting. I was disgusting.

Though completely wrung out, I couldn't leave Spectrum yet; I still had to see my dermatologist. When I showed him my rash that day, he seemed vaguely disapproving of the fact that I hadn't gotten well yet. "I was afraid of this," he said. "There are some people who don't respond to the medication. I guess you're one of them.

"I'm not one-hundred percent convinced you have dermatitis herpitaformis — it *is* rare. But, if you do, I have only two courses: increase your medication or put you on a gluten-free diet. But "I don't recommend the diet. Gluten is in so many foods, it's almost impossible to avoid it. If it's not a main ingredient, it's disguised as an additive."

Still, more medication didn't make sense to me. We'd already increased my dosage twice. If we kept increasing the medication while I continued to eat foods containing wheat, oats, rye, and barley, it seemed about as smart as taking shots of cortisone so I could go out and roll in poison oak!

Getting more overwhelmed by fatigue with every passing minute, wanting only to go home, I asked him to just let me *try* the diet. He gave me a look, then reluctantly retrieved a copy of a gluten-free diet plan from his files and gave it to me — obviously, without his blessing. I'm sure he thought I was determined to do things the hard way. But I'd tried it the so-called easy way already, and I wasn't better. Maybe eliminating gluten would be worth the effort.

I straggled out to my car, almost in tears in my need to get home and lie down. But at least there was good news; I now had two constructive things to do: make new goals and avoid gluten.

After a long nap at home that afternoon, I read the diet plan carefully and began my gluten-free eating that night. The diet may have been the hard way, but it worked. I became a devoted label reader. Within days — whether by happenstance or effect — my rash disappeared. And I was hugely relieved to have one of my torments under control.

Progress. Definitely progress. If only I could go on a despair-free diet, maybe things would be all right. My spirits had lifted, but only the merest fraction of an inch. I was still perilously close to the bottom of the abyss with the Dark Angel of depression dragging on my limbs, reeling me downward, ever downward.

———

One week after I'd originally left L&B on sick leave, I'd decided I should let my friends at the agency know I was okay — even though I wasn't so sure I *was* okay. And I had painstakingly typed up a memo entitled "Superwoman Hangs Up Her Cape," explaining that I needed to take some time off and slow down. Then I mailed the memo to Franklin who had it distributed to the staff.

My co-workers at L&B were good and caring people, and they probably huddled in consultation in the office aisleways wondering about the fate of their fallen comrade. Though I'm sure word had gotten out that I was discouraging phone calls, I still thought it odd that no one tried to get in touch with me, even by mail. First, my birth family, now my work family seemed to be avoiding me. I had heard almost nothing from people at the agency during the entire six weeks I was out on leave.

If I'd had a hysterectomy, my agency friends would probably have sent cards and flowers. If there had been a death in the family, I'm sure they would have offered condolences. But they were probably unsure what Emily Post or Miss Manners would recommend as the appropriate gesture for a co-worker who has simply cracked up.

As enlightened as we may be about health, we are still struggling to bring mental illness out of the shadows of the straw-strewn "insane asylums" of the past and into the light of every day. The term "mental illness" is still weighed down and made pointy-sharp with the stigma of weakness and craziness. We can confront the horrors of cancer with a friend. We can joke about someone's hemorrhoid operation. But a deep depression or other emotional disturbance sends us scurrying for higher ground.

Look at me; I was the patient, armed with facts about the chemical imbalance that precipitated my depression, and I felt as if I'd gone swimming in a sewer. I considered my depression a personal failure. I didn't want to be there with myself during this mess. Was it any wonder my friends from the agency didn't want to be there, either?

Of course, Franklin stayed in touch. He continued to call Larry, trying to find out when I might come back to work. But other than Franklin, performing the necessary truant officer duties, only one person from the agency made any contact with me . . .

Soon after I'd disappeared on sick leave, I received a hand-written note from Jack. In a few short paragraphs he sent his genuine concern. I remember that he urged me to take care of myself, said the job wasn't worth getting sick over. I felt like I was a person to him, not just fodder for the L&B mill. I was touched to know Jack cared enough to write, and I read the note several times.

Eventually, I did hear one bit of office gossip. Word got back to me that the president of L&B in New York, when told one of the copywriters was down for the count in California, had joked with bravado, "Yeah, we like to work people until they have to be carried out on stretchers." I didn't find that funny. I felt like a devalued piece of meat.

Actually, I suppose it was almost easier that most people kept their distance from me. I certainly wasn't up to chatting brightly on the phone. It cost me dearly every time I tried to pretend I was anything but what I was — broken and exhausted.

Not a day went by that I didn't quake in my Reeboks about what lay ahead. I couldn't imagine letting go of L&B but I couldn't imagine how I could hold my fractured body and soul together for even half an hour of a normal day there. When I worried out loud that I *must* get back to work, Larry would shake his head in a disbelieving no. He could not, for the life of him, figure out why I *wanted* to go back. "Annie, Annie," he'd say, "can't you see you're still not well yet? You need to take care of yourself." There was no confrontation; he was just as immovable as Gibraltar. He already regretted he had not done anything months before to prevent me from plummeting into the abyss. And now, by God, he was not going to let me *willingly* jump back in.

Each time I went to see Sherrie, the central topic of our discussion was whether or not I would return to work. I had dutifully completed my goal-setting assignment in my typical hell-bent-for-leatherette fashion. In a new notebook, using construction paper and Magic Markers, I'd created thirteen goal categories, one for each area of my life. Then, in each category, I'd listed a series of new goals.

But in all honesty, I don't think they were really new goals at all. Not new in any sense that would change my life. Different, I suppose, but really just more of the same.

As you'd suspect, the category I gave highest priority in my notebook was "Career" — not "Health," "Spiritual," or "Relationships." The first goal I listed was, "Go back to work at L&B or make an income of sixty-thousand dollars as a free-lancer." I went on to enumerate ten other specific goals for my career — more goals than I was able to come up with for any other section in the notebook. The following week Sherrie read my goals without seeing the underlying message — and I didn't get it, either. My tidy little goal notebook was just another good example of my excellent "motivation."

Finally, in an attempt to help me find a solution to my work dilemma, Sherrie asked me to do a role-playing exercise. First, she had me sit in one chair in her office and talk about going back to work at L&B. Then I had to sit in a chair opposite the first chair and talk about free-lancing instead.

To me, both scenarios sounded dreadful and bleak, as

if the end of my world had come either way. But that's not what Sherrie heard. She told me my manner and voice were strained when I talked about going back to L&B, but that I didn't sound quite as stressed when I talked about free-lancing. Maybe I didn't have complete confidence in Sherrie, but she was all I had. I needed to listen to her, and the plain truth was — much as I hated to admit it — I was afraid I was sucked dry, didn't have the juice to survive at L&B anymore.

One week before my sick leave was officially over, a letter on L&B stationery arrived in the mail. I knew what it must contain. I opened it with the enthusiasm usually reserved for parcels containing ticking devices. The letter was from Franklin. He said they understood my circum-stances, but my sick leave was up and they couldn't wait any longer. I had to let them know if I planned to return to work or resign.

So it had come to this. There were no more tomorrows. I had to decide today whether I was L&B's hotshot copy-writer or just plain shot. I sat down and put the letter on the desk in front of me. With my armored-tank ego and my Duke-self firing salvos of derision all around me, feeling like a weakling and a loser, I picked up the phone and called Victoria. With a minimum of chit-chat, we made an ap-pointment for lunch that Wednesday. On that day I would purportedly tell her what my decision was going to be about returning to work.

But she knew. And I knew. My glory days at L&B were over.

———

On that Wednesday I triple-starched my limp spirits,

slipped into a skinny cotton knit dress, put on gold earrings and high-heeled shoes, and drove to San Francisco to pretend that quitting L&B to free-lance was exactly what I wanted to do. I was a rail, played out with fatigue, with no business walking around out in the world. But this, I thought, was how a professional should handle quitting.

For the first time in almost seven weeks I climbed the wide brick steps of the L&B building. Before entering, I stood for a moment in front of the brass-trimmed double doors of what was soon to be my past. I took a breath the size and weight of a boulder and tugged my guts up out of my shoes.

Elevator to the third floor. Doors opening on blood-red carpeting. Art on the walls. A ceramic vase with a fortune in cut flowers on the front desk. Fancy lobby furniture. Leafy indoor trees. Nothing's changed, I thought. Except everything.

I felt like a visitor from another planet. It didn't seem right just to stroll on back to Victoria's office, and I knew I wasn't up to making infinitely small talk with any old friends who might be working through lunch. So I asked the receptionist to ring Victoria and tell her I was waiting in the lobby.

Within a few minutes Victoria breezed into view. Turned out in her usual high fashion and fourteen-karat charm, Victoria awed me as always. Her upbeat welcome-back greeting struck me as genuine — but also shockingly nonchalant. I guessed her aim was to keep this light. And we were off.

The restaurant we'd chosen was just two blocks away. We walked the distance in the warm sunlight of early September, talking about I don't know what. We sat down at a snowy cloth-draped table crammed with glassware, heavy bistro china and flatware, looked over the menu, and ordered.

As Victoria chatted, I was having to pull myself up hand-over-hand from fifty-thousand leagues beneath my skin just to be there with her. For the first few minutes I was waiting for her to ask me how I was. But that was the one subject she seemed to be artfully avoiding. She talked about the latest creative projects at the agency, her upcoming vacation, news of the staff. I wore my happy face and dredged up stock enthusiasms to pretend I was still a person who had a life.

Looking back, I realize how ironic that lunch was. I was trying so hard to appear lifelike and normal — yet it was incomprehensible to me that I might be pulling it off. How could Victoria believe I was okay? Surely she could see through my I'm-okay facade to the wreck I actually was. I didn't bring up my weeks of depression because it seemed impolite, like vomiting on the table. But I didn't for one minute believe Victoria was buying my smiling mannequin face. I thought she just didn't want to be exposed to any of the messy little details of my life.

But I had nothing else in my life *except* that depression. While Victoria carried the conversation with anecdotes, interesting happenings, tales of the advertising world and beyond, I felt like a dead person. I had nothing to contribute. I had no amusing stories. I had no laughter or life left in me. I was dizzy and disoriented just trying to keep up as Victoria scattered a confetti of words.

Throughout lunch I kept hauling up my bootstraps, telling myself to quit feeling sorry for myself. Then I suddenly remembered something I felt good about. Pleased I'd been able to think of even one positive thing about my life in these dark days, I told Victoria, "I've been doing a lot of walking; I've worked up to two miles a day."

Without realizing the significance my statement held for me, Victoria said, "Oh, I'm *running* six miles a day!" Without meaning to, she swept my one small success off the table, like so many dried-up bread crumbs.

I felt as if I'd been slugged with a two-by-four.

The rest of lunch I was blurry with emotion. After the waiter delivered the check on a little black plastic tray, I told Victoria I wouldn't be coming back to L&B. As I'd guessed, Victoria already knew. She told me she was sorry and that she'd save me lots of free-lance work. But I felt as if I'd cut out my heart and left it on the table.

Half an hour later, in the car on the way home, I began to replay the whole lunch in my thoughts, worrying its frayed edges with the fingers of my mind. When I got to the part where Victoria said, "I'm *running* six miles a day!", I was no longer sad. I was angry.

What the hell were these people — my so-called friends at the agency, Victoria especially — thinking of? Why hadn't they expressed any concern for me all these weeks? Didn't they care I'd gone down in emotional flames? You had to say you *ran* six miles, Victoria? When I'm telling you I'm trying to learn to walk?

I had no idea Victoria really hadn't seen through to the broken, ruined Ann at that lunch; I only thought she didn't care. It was four more years before Victoria revealed how my collapse had driven her to an ocean beach. On the day I'd called her sobbing, saying I had to take some time off, Victoria was so upset she left the office. She drove to a deserted beach and stayed there for hours staring at the crashing waves, wrestling with her concern and her guilt.

When Victoria went home from the beach that day,

she talked with her husband, still worrying that my break-down was something she should have seen coming. Something she might have helped to prevent. For my always bright and shining, inscrutable boss, that dark admission said a lot.

All those years later, I was glad to know. Oh, if only in the business of daily life we dared to be as warm and compassionate as we really are!

All those years later, Victoria also told me how relieved she'd been at our last lunch when I appeared so well, calm, even happy about my decision to leave the agency. Whether that was the tranquilizing effect of my antidepressants or Victoria's own desire to see me well, I don't know. Either way, it was a lying mask. My truest self was behind that mask weeping, weeping for the loss of my self-respect and my job.

On Friday of the week I resigned, I took a small cardboard box to the L&B office and gathered up the things I had accumulated over my two-and-a-half years as an L&B copywriter. After I'd cleaned out my desk, I went around to all my friends to say good-bye. They joshed with me about getting-out-while-the-getting-was-good, gave me hugs and best wishes, and said they wished they could get away to free-lance, too. But I knew none of them envied the reason I was going to be so unattached and free.

Finally, I'd said all my good-byes except for Franklin; he'd asked me to come and see him just before I left. When we were alone in his office, Franklin said, "So this is it . . . we're going to miss you around here. Clients have been asking about you. People in the industry may be wondering why you're leaving, too. Of course, we need to tell them something . . ." And there, he paused.

"I think it would be better if we didn't say anything to anyone about your getting sick . . . Why don't you and I just agree to tell people that you're going back to free-lancing so you can spend more time with your family and pursue your community interests?"

A part of me chuckled a secret, sad little laugh. So this was why he wanted to see me. So the L&B name would not be besmirched. Okay, Franklin, I told him. It's okay to tell everybody that . . . and don't worry, Franklin, I won't tell anyone it's L&B's fault.

I knew my depression *wasn't* L&B's fault. Maybe I'd been a genetic time bomb just waiting to go off. Maybe I was foolish and naive enough never to say no. Franklin didn't need to worry because I wasn't leaving armed with bitterness and blame. I had loved L&B. *But Franklin*, I thought, *wouldn't you at least like to tell me to have a good life?*

I carried the box of mementos and just-plain-stuff down to my car and drove home on the undulating meander of the I-280 freeway. I made the trip on automatic pilot, for really the greater part of me was packed away in that small cardboard box on the back seat. My star had been taken from the door, from the very heavens.

What was that sound? Only the slow crash of my dreams.

7

Land
of the
Living Dead

*S*TOP. *Go back. Return
to START and begin again.*

That's the card I'd drawn in the game of life. But I
refused to accept it. I shoved it back into the very bottom of
the pile, determined to play on.

When I think back on my actions during those next
few months, I realize I was clinging to an unconscious
game plan drawn up years before — a plan from which I
refused to vary, no matter how much circumstances
changed. This game plan called for me to perform according to standards that I now recognize as dictated by Duke —
my inner masculine. Unfettered by reality or the facts, his
game plan predetermined what I should accomplish or do
with my life, what kind of person I should be.

For all of my thirty-eight years, I'd bought into that
plan, tacked up an eight-by-ten glossy of a perfect, idealized

Ann-person on my wall and constantly measured myself against her. Actually, that Ann-person wasn't perfect at all. She was just a cardboard, preconceived notion of who I thought Ann was. And without realizing it, I was basing my one and only real life on what I thought that made-up Ann would do, be, think, or have.

Though unaware of it, I was living under a tyranny of I-AMs and I-MUSTs. I MUST be strong . . . I AM cooperative . . . I MUST work hard . . . I AM understanding and loving at all times . . . I MUST be pretty and fun to be with . . . I AM weak; therefore I MUST be vigilant against weakness . . . I AM a copywriter . . . I MUST never be sick . . . I MUST sleep at night, never nap, never be tired . . . I MUST be witty and upbeat . . . I MUST get the job done no matter what the cost . . . I MUST take care of other people and earn my keep. And on. And on. In every area of my life.

Of course, this tyranny of I-AMs and I-MUSTs didn't make me that much different from anyone else. Although few of us realize it, most of us fall into the covert but deadly I-AM/I-MUST ego trap, becoming prisoners of our own ideas about ourselves. But, in my case, there was a problem with clinging to such a rigid self-image: I was experiencing some technical difficulties in acting out the Ann-person I'd dreamed up. My body had jerked me up short. I was having trouble living up to my "healthy, successful, hardworking" ideals because my body and my reality weren't cooperating.

When I think back on my turmoil at the end of 1983, I'm reminded of an experiment I read about years ago. As I remember it, the experiment involved a monkey and a gourd (or it may have been a hollow log or a coconut.) The researcher cut a small hole in the gourd, making the hole large enough for a monkey to reach inside, but not large enough to allow the monkey to withdraw its closed fist.

Inside the small opening in the gourd, the researcher tucked a tasty tidbit no monkey could resist. Then he placed the gourd where the monkey would find it and watched to see what would happen. High levels of monkey frustration ensued. The monkey reached greedily for the treat, then screeched and ranted, refusing to let go of his prize, at the same time raging at being trapped by the gourd.

In 1983 I was no smarter than that monkey. Freedom would be mine only if I could let go. What was being asked of me now seems so simple. All I needed to do was work out an erasable new game plan, burn the eight-by-ten glossy, and become more authentically Ann. Give it up. Give in. Acquiesce. Instead, I clung all the more fiercely to my tattered old plan and my glossified image. And, as a result, I could not be creative or loving or responsive to the tough situation in which I found myself.

How should I have taken care of myself? What was the healthiest choice I could have made regarding work? *How could I possibly have known?* I was blinded, hobbled, and mummified by my cast-iron concepts about life and myself.

According to my scheme of things, being idle was a sin, or at the very least a venal embarrassment. I could not look on being freed from my job as the blessed opportunity for healing it surely was. Instead, I viewed my days as a wasteland. I was afraid to "do nothing" because then I felt I would be worthless. I didn't want to be an invalid, which was just another way of saying in-valid, to me. If I gave into ill health, I might never get on my feet again. Recovery, I thought, must be brought about by an act of will. And I willed to carry on.

I was a wraith, a sick and tottery house-of-cards woman. But I refused to succumb; that's what I called it, succumbing. I was going to be strong, put my breakdown behind me, and resume a so-called normal life.

So, just two weeks after I resigned from L&B, I purchased a black leather portfolio, carefully selected my best advertising samples, tucked them into the portfolio, and went out to look for free-lance work.

It wasn't difficult to get appointments to show my book to agencies and clients — just a phone call here, a few announcement letters there. After all, there still weren't that many direct marketing copywriters around, and I was what I called a "graduate" of the highly respected L&B.

On the days I'd booked appointments, I'd be dimly recaptured by the old advertising thrill, however spectrally. I'd get my scarecrow body all dressed up, put on my shopworn happy face, cart my book into someone's office geared up as if for battle, and win a copy assignment. But it wasn't really a win. The cost was enormous. In the car on the way home, I'd end up sobbing with battle fatigue. I was so drained I didn't know how, how in the world I was going to be able to write a single word of the copy I'd just won the chance to write. (But I AM a copywriter; I MUST carry on.)

During that fall and winter, I dutifully took my antidepressants, but doubts encompassed me. From what I could tell, the only value of my medication was its ability to help me sleep (however groggily) and eat (however joylessly). Other than that, the small balloon of hope I'd experienced upon diagnosis was steadily deflating. I began to suspect I was *never* going to be well again. Hopelessness crept back in to germinate like toadstools in my darkening interior. And slowly, slowly I settled into a routine of despair.

Everything I did, I did out of duty. There was no joy left even in my work. My creativity withered and left me, like dead leaves drifting away down empty streets deserted for all time. I was so spiritless and empty that when I did write, it was in a manner that reminded me of the last stages of giving birth — pushing, pushing, pushing; forcing out words and ideas until I was utterly exhausted from the labor.

Even the most everyday activities required grinding effort, and I soon learned to avoid the shopping center altogether. No matter how rested I thought I was or how inconsequential the errand seemed, the mall was always draining — too many people, too much confusion and noise, too many choices for my muddled brain.

Besides, a trip to the mall was usually followed by a demoralizing case of the Blue Envies. All those women — pushing babies in strollers, trundling armloads of packages, dashing in after their tennis lessons — their faces blooming with color, the lights on in their eyes. They seemed so robust, so unaware of their own good health. And I was so jealous. What was I doing wrong that I couldn't be rosy, energetic and happy like that? By comparison, I felt like a cadaver with my organs removed and my body fluids drained.

I was sick in body and spirit. I was living without life or hope. Just plodding, plodding on. I had entered The Land of the Living Dead.

———

Through October, November, December, I forced myself to write and cook and do the laundry. I forced myself to talk at the dinner table. I forced myself to keep up a semblance of a normal life. And I forced myself to continue seeing Sherrie once a week at Spectrum. I went to the sessions but felt like I was on a grindingly slow-motion merry-go-round. Sherrie and I seemed to go on and on about nothing, accomplishing nothing, as far as I was concerned.

If my depression was chemical, why weren't the anti-depressants making a bigger difference? If it was psycho-logical, why weren't my sessions with Sherrie more help-ful? I hated being depressed, despised it, raged against being pinned down by my Dark Angel. But there seemed to be no escape.

During one of my medication appointments with Dr. Wong, I asked him, "Do you think I'm crazy?" Dr. Wong laughed easily at such a crazy notion, then saw I was serious.

"No, of course not. Here, I'll prove it. What's today's date?"

November 22, 1983.

"Who's the President of the United States?"

Ronald Reagan.

"How much is six times four, plus two, plus fifteen, minus six, plus nine?"

Forty-four.

Boy, if that's all it took to be sane, the world was a pretty shaky place.

Wasn't there someone somewhere who had been through a suicidal depression and lived to tell the story? If only I could find such a person and sit down for a long talk. Oh, how I needed someone who'd been there to tell me it was possible to make it back. At that time the only person I knew who had suffered from deep depression was my dad — and he had *not* made it back.

In the newspaper, on bulletin boards, in hospital news-letters, I saw notices of support groups for cancer patients, manic depressives, anorexics, alcoholics, single parents, all kinds of suffering humans. Was there a support group for people who were chemically depressed? No one seemed to know of any such group — except group therapy inside psychiatric hospitals. Would it help to sit around weeping in unison in a circle of fellow sufferers? I didn't know, but at least I might not feel so alien and alone.

Was there a book that told the story of someone who'd experienced a deep depression and recovered? I didn't want to read some Ph.D.'s or M.D.'s treatise on mental illness. I didn't want to read some upbeat, know-it-all best seller on how to say bye-bye to the blues. I needed a blood-and-guts real story about a survivor. I searched my public library, turning up only two out-of-date volumes about people who'd had shock therapy. My father had shock treatments — but thousands of volts hadn't made him well. The only book in which I found "hope" was the dictionary.

In spite of the antidepressants and the therapy, I began once more to spiral down . . . then Christmas descended in on top of me. Shopping, decorating the tree, wrapping presents, baking, trying to manufacture holiday spirit — I didn't see how I could do it. But I thought I MUST.

When I saw Dr. Wong in December and told him I'd reached the end of my tinsel string, he assured me that thousands of people battle black tides of depression during the holidays. Once again, he increased my medication. And I ground on.

My mother called me as often as she dared that winter, not wanting me to think she was worrying about me, though I knew she was. Each time she called, I wanted so much to be able to say, "Mom, I'm all better." But I obviously was not.

My mother also sent long, loving letters. In an effort to encourage me and keep my spirits up, she searched out scriptures she thought might help. She did all these things cautiously, not trusting herself, not wanting to interfere or offend me. Finally, in one letter she offered the suggestion that maybe I should try to "get outside myself" and "do something for someone else."

I immediately recognized the helping-others idea as a tried-and-true remedy for the blues. A wave of shame rolled over me because the tried-and-true assumption seemed to be that depressions stemmed from pure, unadulterated self-pity. But I decided I might as well give the theory a try. Nothing else was working.

The day after receiving my mother's letter, I called the local volunteer center and made an appointment to find out what kinds of jobs were available. Later, in the center's offices, I leafed through a binder thick with sheets of paper listing all the possible volunteer options. Reeling with indecision, I told the coordinator I'd try assisting at the local food bank before I made my final choice.

On the appointed day I grimly joined the other volunteers packing donated foodstuffs into used shopping bags, which were then picked up by needy people from the community. I'll tell you a secret: Helping others may be good for the blues, but it is *not* a cure for deep depression. What I needed to do first of all was help myself. Volunteerism lasted two weeks.

As for those closest to me, John and Larry were my blessings. John went about the business of being fourteen the best he could. While he could easily have fallen in with the party-till-you-puke crowd, just to escape the painful times at home, he did not. Instead, he focused his attention on soul music, soccer, swimming, skateboarding, a few well-chosen friends, and, occasionally, his homework.

While John never was able or willing to discuss his feelings about my depression, I knew he was listening and observing every minute of every day — listening to and observing his father's extraordinary example. As the months passed, John, like Larry, proved able to love me even as deconstructed as I was. I can remember the times John would hug me and say, "I love you, Mom." Sometimes he even succeeded in making his aching-hearted mom laugh. And it felt so good. To both of us. (Oh, how we missed laughing!)

I mourned what John was growing up with; I knew all too well what it was like to be a teenager living in a household draped in the black crepe of depression. But John held his own and developed a heart of sensitivity and compassion that will be one of his best gifts to the world.

And how would I have made it through a single day of those long months without Larry? When I was so exhausted and afraid that I cried the night away, when I woke with dread for the desolation of the coming day, when my sexual desire was only a memory, Larry just accepted the hard realities, believed in my recovery, and loved me. He was like a life preserver. Something steady, tangible, and secure in the rough seas of depression.

Some days my tired, unbidden tears welled up and came leaking out before breakfast, before I even got out of bed. Larry, freshly showered and shaved, would come to me, put his arms around me, and tell me, "I know it's really rough. But you're going to get well. You're going to get better and better every day." We'd look at each other for a long moment, then he'd kiss me with love and compassion, and leave for work.

I know to some people it may seem callous that Larry

could walk away from his shattered, weeping wife and go to his job. They might expect a true hero would have fretted over me, cried with me, wrung his hands a little, gotten me a babysitter, torn up his own life. But in truth that would have been neither heroic nor healthy.

To me, Larry's being able to go to work was an act of faith and confidence. I found strength in the fact that Larry was not afraid to leave me; he was always tender and loving without once taking away my self-respect and power. To him, I was not a victim. It was evident that Larry believed what he said: I was going to be all right. I clutched his words and his belief like a lifeline.

———

During that long winter, I hauled myself through each day dragging my ball and chain of fatigue. I was so tired that brushing my teeth became an aerobic activity. My voice was husky, my speech slow and full of effort. If slumbering could be rightly defined as it sounds, an unrestful and oppressive combination of sleeping and lumbering, that's what I did: I slumbered. Each morning I woke feeling drugged, as if I had to crawl up out of a pit to greet the day. And to the day facing me I said, "I have nothing left for you."

Before my medication, my depression was sharp and spiky, fraught with terror, anxiety, and anarchy. After my medication, everything just went flat and empty. Still I kept trying to act as if nothing had happened, slaving to uphold my I-AMs and I-MUSTs, and working to keep my free-lancing career alive.

I especially remember one terrible business meeting, sitting at a big oak conference table with three agency representatives and their client. I didn't want to be there, or anywhere. From way inside myself I watched as the others argued heatedly, even passionately — they actually cared — whether the envelopes should be white or blue. I sat in silence contemplating razor blades and suicide.

The weeks ground on; life ground on. More and more often, I thought of suicide. Not making any specific sharp-edged or powdery plans, only considering that it might be a better option than the death I was currently living.

Larry knew the turn my thoughts were taking and threatened to call Sherrie and Dr. Wong himself, though I'm not sure what he thought he might accomplish. He never wavered in his belief that I was going to "get better and better every day," but he was not going to be lulled into complacency this time, either.

Despair crept up and up like flood water, filling every cell of my body to the limits of capacity until it overflowed in an aching deluge. And still more despair poured in.

———

It was December 31, 1983. Seven months had now passed since I had crashed-and-burned on "The Day of the Bagel." It was the night to ring in a new year. And if anyone needed a new year, I did.

Larry and I had never been wild about New Year's Eve parties. An evening of so-how-do-you-know-the-host/hostess conversations, followed by the prospect of sloppy, sentimental kisses from unlikely strangers whose holiday spirits came bottled, was not one of our favorite things to do. And, for obvious reasons, on the eve of 1984 Larry and I were even less likely than usual to put on our high-heeled sneakers and carouse till the tiny hours. What seemed more appropriate for us was to have a quiet evening at home, skip the Guy Lombardo music and the ball dropping on

Times Square, and go to bed at a reasonable hour, kissing only each other.

That New Year's Eve, before Larry arrived home from work and his nightly racquetball match, the house was quiet and dark except for lights in the kitchen and dining room where I was getting things ready for dinner. I was alone; John had left early to celebrate New Year's with his friends.

The silence of the house was broken when the automatic garage door opener ground into operation, shaking the house. A car door slammed shut down below in the garage, the garage door opener ground again, and Larry came up the stairs two at a time. In the entry hall he drew me to him, squeezed me in a happy hug, and twirled me around in just the way I've always loved.

"There's something I want you to hear," he said. He shushed me with his finger to his lips and went straight to the stereo cabinet, turned on one small light in the darkened living room and began searching through our seldom-played collection of old record albums. Smiling, he found what he was looking for, withdrew the record from its jacket, placed it on the turntable, and put the needle at ready.

Coming back to me, he put his arm around me, led me into the almost-dark living room, and had me sit down on the couch. "I want you to listen to this," he said. "Just listen."

Larry crossed the room to the stereo cabinet again and set the needle down on the record. Then, in the quiet before the first note sang from the speakers, he came to sit beside me on the couch. In a moment the intimate, reassuring words of Paul Simon's "Bridge Over Troubled Water" flowed around me. Time stopped, and I listened with my very soul.

As many times as I'd heard this pop classic, I had never heard the words in this way before. The song washed over me like liquid silver. I cried, only this time it was tears that had a hint of breathing freshness.

As we sat holding onto each other in the dark and the silence after the song was over, Larry said he had heard the song on an oldies radio station on the way home, and he wanted to remind me that, if I needed a friend, he would always, always, be sailing right behind me. He wanted me to know I was his "silvergirl" and I could make it.

I was still so sad and wrecked, but how could I not get well when someone loved me like this? If I was at the bottom of the black abyss, Larry was standing on the edge above, letting down a little rope ladder of love. Surely, even as far down as I was, even as fragile as that ladder was, there must be a way I could climb it.

8

The Only
Way Out
Is Through

*I*t was a tarnished "silvergirl" who opened the Yellow Pages the following week, slowly running her finger down the columns in the "Counselor" section, searching for a new therapist. A weary but willing silvergirl with one elbow on the desk and her head propped in her hand.

If I was going to get better and better every day, as Larry believed, I knew I had to shake things up. I was beginning to realize that the only way out of my depression was going to be *through* my fear, *through* my confusion, *through* untried and unexplored aspects of myself. I couldn't detour around what I did not like; I had to encounter the reality of my life and work *with* it.

For whatever reason, my therapy at Spectrum had not clicked. I hadn't felt any connection with Sherrie at the beginning, and the gulf between us hadn't diminished one centimeter in the seven months since. While I'm sure Sherrie's reticence was a healing balm for many of her clients, she was not the right therapist for me. But it was not an easy decision to go my own way.

In the first place, if I left Sherrie and Spectrum, I worried I might be copping out, blaming my problems and my failure to come out of this depression on other people. Leaving would be like saying my therapy isn't working, and it's *their* fault. But I didn't really believe that.

What I did believe was this: Relationships are built on warmth and love, mutual respect, and richness of communication. That's what I valued in my everyday relationships. Why should I expect less in my relationship with someone as important as a therapist?

Second, I squirmed at the idea I might be searching for Mr. or Ms. Right Therapist out of some demented notion I was *special*. Maybe I was just a pain-in-the-butt person who had to have things her own way, someone who thought she needed special treatment all the time. Spectrum had a system; why couldn't I just fit into it like everybody else?

Well, special or not, there was no denying that my therapy wasn't working at Spectrum. Maybe I did have to have things my own way, even if that meant being ultra nit-picky about a therapist.

And I had one final concern about leaving Spectrum. A monumental matter of dollars and cents. Because Spectrum was an HMO, our insurance coverage extended only to physicians, services, and therapists within the Spectrum organization. If I wanted to choose a therapist outside Spectrum, we would have to pay the therapist's fees entirely out of our own pocket — perhaps as much as two hundred dollars a week for months to come. Though Larry chafed at the burden this would place on the family budget, he wanted me to do whatever I needed to get well.

There was no way around it; private therapy was going to cost a lot of money. But I tried to think of it as an investment in myself, my own futures market. There was no guaranteed return on this investment, but it was a financial risk I had to take. If it paid off, my returns would be slow, steady gains in my health and happiness, and a normal family life. There was nothing in the material world I wanted more than that.

My mind pointed an accusing finger at me, chiding me for spending so much money on myself — I MUST not be selfish; I MUST be a nice person. But I was beginning to question the eight-by-ten glossy Ann and that cherished game plan. I believed I must do something constructive, even if it didn't fit my image of myself. And I must do it *now*. In the doing, I touched a small flame to the old carry-on-at-all-costs cardboard Ann and began my real life.

That's how I came to the point of scanning the columns of therapists' names in our phone book, wondering how I was going to narrow down this list of possibilities to a few good prospects. I knew I could not afford to simply settle for the nearest, cheapest, or most available person, so I decided to see if any of the listings stood out — mentioning depression or stress, for example. In addition to that, I decided I would ask people I knew for personal referrals.

No matter how I got the names, I vowed to *audition* my potential therapists, try them out for a few sessions before deciding if the situation was right for me. And I would hold out until I found someone with whom I felt a real connection. Someone I trusted and thought to be wise. Preferably someone with wit and the good sense to use it.

I know this sounds as if, by January, I had miraculously

become self-possessed and analytical — as if I were humming along, my troubles essentially over, plans forming easily in my mind. But that's an inaccurate picture. In truth, my brain was sludge, my energy nonexistent. I grappled with the problem of finding a therapist because I could not bear my life as it was; necessity was the mother of intervention.

———

The first phone book listing that attracted my attention was a professional ad for a woman Ph.D. who had an office in a neighboring suburb. The ad mentioned dream analysis, and the idea of having an expert work with me on interpreting these messages from the unconscious had always fascinated me. So I called and made an appointment.

But after two sessions with this therapist, I began to feel uneasy. I was still struggling with black and suicidal thoughts and was worried that therapy focusing on dreams and symbols lacked concreteness and specificity. Because I felt I wasn't tacked down in any way, that was frightening. What I thought I needed was the therapeutic equivalent of ropes, nets, tent pegs, anchors, and ten-penny nails to keep me from being borne away on great black wings of despair.

Still, I might have worked through my fear of investing everything in that free-floating inner journey and accomplished great things with this therapist. But something got in my way besides fear. At one of those early sessions, when I began to cry, my therapist leaped from her chair, rushed to my side, knelt down beside me with a handful of Kleenex, and said with woeful concern, "Oh, you're having such a hard time; there, there."

I had enough woeful concern of my own. I didn't need a therapist's, too. I felt myself become prickly and inaccessible, shrinking from that kind of "help." Being helped in that way made me feel helpless, less-than, scared for myself, like a real mess. I wanted compassion, empathy, and objectivity from a therapist, not sympathy and professional hand wringing. No, this person would not do. And that ended my trial period with the lady Ph.D.

When I quit seeing that therapist, I wasn't without a counseling base. Until I could work out an alternate therapy plan, I was continuing to see Sherrie once a week. I did not want to revert to not eating or sleeping, so I thought I would have to stay in the good graces of Spectrum in order to get my antidepressants. I simply considered my sessions at Spectrum treading water. And I continued to search for a therapist/lifeguard who could teach me how to swim.

Fortunately, I didn't have to search much further than my own address book.

———

About two years before, when John was having trouble making his way through the social and academic briar patch of junior high school, some friends of ours had suggested a local clinical psychologist, Dr. Alfred Fricke. These parents recommended Dr. Fricke highly, based on their own son's recent experience with counseling. John saw Dr. Fricke a few times, and Larry and I met with him twice. During those sessions we found Dr. Fricke to be both an insightful therapist and a very likeable person.

I didn't think Dr. Fricke worked with adult clients, but I decided to call him and at least ask. If he didn't work with adult clients, I hoped he could recommend another therapist he knew personally. I phoned Dr. Fricke's office and left my name and phone number with his answering service. Within two hours, he called back. "Ann, Al Fricke here.

How's John?" he greeted me, naturally assuming John was the reason for my call.

I told him John was fine, but his mother was not. In an overstuffed nutshell — in the ten minutes between his last appointment and the arrival of his next — I explained to Dr. Fricke about my breakdown and unremitting depression. Hardly daring to take time to breathe for fear we'd be out of time, I plunged on asking if he took adult clients (yes), if he had experience working with depression (yes), and if he had any openings in his schedule (yes to that, too).

The joke was I thought I was interviewing Dr. Fricke, but actually he was interviewing me. Dr. Fricke later told me he listens very carefully when people call to discuss starting therapy and then asks himself: Is this a person with whom I'd work well? Would I enjoy this association? He said no matter what his schedule looks like, he accepts only clients with whom he thinks he can create a mutually rewarding working relationship. (That was the first of many practical things I would learn from Dr. Fricke about work and self-respect.)

I guess Dr. Fricke loved a challenge or was intrigued by the idea of working with a client who had swapped her sense of humor for a rain of tears, because he knew all about me, and he still took me on. We made an appointment for the end of the following week, his first available time slot. How I wished I could fast-forward time to that day.

When I walked into Dr. Fricke's waiting room eight days later, everything looked the same as two years before. Same church pew staging area, same wildly colorful parrot print on the drapes, same bright green carpeting. Only the magazines were different. I punched the buzzer that let Dr. Fricke know I had arrived and sat down on the narrow church pew — for me, a kind of unconscious reminder to say a prayer that now at last I might really get well.

When Dr. Fricke came out to get me, he looked as welcoming and receptive as I'd remembered from the last time. He was garbed in his usual therapist uniform: muted plaid sportscoat, casual slacks, permanent press shirt, undershirt, no tie, and suede Hush Puppy shoes. He wore dark-framed glasses, had brown not-too-long-or-short hair parted on the side, smiled easily, and radiated good vibes. There was something about him that always reminded me of a little boy who might read adventure books during church, a good kid with just enough snips, snails, puppy dog tails, and cherry bombs to make life interesting and fun.

Once I'd followed Dr. Fricke into his office, I noticed it looked the same, too — the overburdened bookshelves, the arched wicker étagère, a small ceramic sculpture done by one of his three daughters, and an assortment of games he played with his younger clients so he could observe them in action. I hoped I didn't have to shoot any Nerf basketball with him.

Dr. Fricke walked over to his chair, which was pushed away from his desk at one end of the room. I looked around, picked out a chair, and sat down. Dr. Fricke had furnished his office with two overstuffed chairs, two wooden captain's chairs, and two upholstery-and-chrome-tubing office chairs. These seats were scattered around the room at various distances from Dr. Fricke's own. I often wondered how much he learned about his clients based on which chairs they chose and how far away from him they sat. I chose the absolutely closest seat and would have been happier if the toes of our shoes had been touching. I hadn't anticipated it, but seeing Dr. Fricke was like coming home to an old friend.

I wish I could tell you specifically what happened at that first session with Dr. Fricke, but I can't. All I can remember is how heavy with depression I felt, how scared, how needy, how grasping for hope. I, of course, cried and sobbed, telling him all the details of my collapse, using up the Kleenex strategically placed beside my chair. But this time I didn't have to deal with a leaping therapist. Dr. Fricke didn't say, "There, there." Instead, he just listened and allowed me to experience what I was experiencing.

Actually, I can't remember much at all about that first session, except the most important thing: Once, in the middle of my recounting all this suffering, Dr. Fricke said something that made me laugh! I was startled and cheered by the sound of my own laughter. It was better medicine than seven months of antidepressants. Mentally and emotionally I bought all available shares of Dr. Fricke's stock and put them in my name. Here's where I was going to get well. Right here in this room with its topsy-turvy bookshelves, Nerf basketball hoop, foam rubber "boffing sticks" clients used for bopping out their aggressions, and a soccer boardgame leaning up against the wall.

To this day, I find it truly miraculous that even after all those months of depression, even though my chest was at that moment weighed down by despair, I still felt myself lifting up toward hope again. The human spirit has the wings of a phoenix, I am sure.

However, it must have been clear to Dr. Fricke what a precarious and shaky state I was in. At the end of the session, he pulled out his appointment book and asked, "What would you think about coming in two times a week?" I thought two sessions a week sounded fine. Seven days a week, twice a day would have sounded even better. Actually, I would have preferred to camp out in his office. To me, those appointments were like ice floes, and I was Little Nell crossing the wintry river, lurching from one semisecure chunk of ice to the next, trying to make my way toward the safety of shore. But, okay, two appointments a week would have to do. So we went ahead and scheduled time slots for the next two weeks.

Instead of fifty minutes, I wished that first session could have lasted fifty hours. But when my time was up, I left reluctantly through the discreet outside door of Dr. Fricke's inner office — discreet, because I didn't have to pass by other clients in the waiting room on my way out with my emotions written in mascara all over my face. And behind me I left an imaginary trail of bread crumbs so I could find my way back to the little bit of security and hope I had found in Dr. Fricke's office full of chairs.

I felt sure now that I had found my therapist-of-choice, and I let Sherrie know what I had decided to do and that I would not be coming back. But there was still the matter of my antidepressants.

The following week, in my regularly scheduled medication appointment with Dr. Wong, I told him about my decision to begin therapy with Dr. Fricke. Then I explained that the problem was that Dr. Fricke was not a psychiatrist but a psychologist, and so could not prescribe antidepressants.

Surprisingly, Dr. Wong seemed impassive on the subject of my ending my therapy with Sherrie. He said if that's what I wanted to do, he could still go on being my prescribing physician. All I had to do was continue to make once-a-month medication appointments so he could monitor my progress. We agreed that was exactly what I would do.

———

Though I now had what I hoped was a veteran scout and guide for the trek out of the Land of the Living Dead, I was a desperate woman. Exhausted and barely able to function, I continued to try to work, but I was at the end of any kind of coping at all. Within those first two or three weeks of therapy, I was again swept under by a wave of hopelessness. Again, suicide seemed the only escape from unending misery and despair.

In Dr. Fricke's office I cried and cried. I said I wanted to kill myself, that I didn't have an ounce of anything left to give to life. He listened carefully and asked if I had any reason at all to live, any reason *not* to kill myself. The only reason I could think of was that I didn't want to cause Larry, John, and my mother pain and grief. Dr. Fricke said, "Well, keeping yourself alive for someone else is at least a start."

He took out a pad of paper, pulled his chair right up next to mine, and wrote: I, Ann Keiffer, agree not to harm myself in any way, either accidentally or on purpose.

"We need to talk about making an agreement," he said, holding the pad so I could see what he'd written. "Can you agree not to do anything to yourself for a month?"

I was crying. What he was asking seemed so simple, but I didn't think I could promise that. Slowly I shook my head, sobbing, no.

"How about two weeks?"

More weeping. I could not promise two weeks. Once

more I shook my head, no.

"One week?"

A long, sniffling pause. Could I promise that? Finally, again, no.

"What is the longest time you could promise?" he asked.

Still crying, I thought for several minutes, and said, "Two days." I believed I could hold on that long; it was the number of days until my next appointment.

With his pen Dr. Fricke completed the statement so it read: "I, Ann Keiffer, agree not to harm myself in any way, either accidentally or on purpose, for the next two days." He handed me the paper and the pen, and I signed my name.

I did make it through the two days until our next session, and at that session I agreed not to harm myself for the five days until I would see Dr. Fricke again. My third agreement was for a week. By the following week, I was able to make an agreement that did not have any ending date at all.

Though I was still tottery and grim, I was able to slog on. We were traveling slowly out of the wilderness in a series of hard, uphill day journeys.

———

For months I had suspected that my journey out of depression might be connected to my need for a life of the spirit — not the dogma of organized religion necessarily, but a personal experience of God, a deeper meaning for my life. The problem was, my girlhood God was stuck somewhere back in Sunday School, not very accessible to a grown woman in deep trouble.

Empty and longing, I began to visit churches in early 1984, making a pew-by-pew search for a Creative and Loving God, One in whom I could "live and move and have my being." But it turned out to be a disheartening expedition for a bleeding-heart liberal like me, especially as my heart was then bleeding rivulets of despair.

In the first church the minister preached his sermon on the "troubling" news that Catholics were taking over in Central America. In the second, the clergyman performed the ritual of baptism for "sinful" little babies who looked as innocent as, well, babies to me. In the third, the congregation was working on its "prosperity consciousness" and beseeching God for freely flowing cash and new Chevies. In the fourth, my favorite old hymns had been rewritten, and Jesus had become just a pretty nice guy. In the fifth, the congregation worshipped a God who'd hold a grudge for all eternity if you didn't follow every humanly impossible rule. And in the sixth, the air was so dry and dusty and stagnant, it seemed the church had died.

I hauled my depression from sanctuary to sanctuary, but found no sanctuary. I was a spiritual misfit and went away all the more depressed that I could not embrace these churches or feel embraced by them. Maybe I'd come at a bad time, and God wasn't in right then. Actually, God was in. In the one place I hadn't looked yet; in the depths of depression.

————

I didn't like who I was. I didn't see how it would ever be possible for me to love the stay-at-home, weeping, and sick person I had become. All I could feel for myself was judgment and disgust made all the more bitter by hopelessness. To Larry, I said, "Am I still getting better and better every day?" And his answer was still, incomprehensibly and unequivocally, yes.

In my sessions with Dr. Fricke, I was impatient. I strained for solutions, wanted to hurry up the process, coveted the time when I could take a "real job" again. To Dr. Fricke, I said, "I'd give anything to get back to the way I was."

Dr. Fricke was gently amused; he smiled from experience and said, "You know, people always sit in that chair and say, 'I want to get back to the way I used to be.' They forget that being the way they used to be is what got them into trouble in the first place."

On another occasion I was wrestling with the question, "Why me?" and Dr. Fricke said, "I have this image of you tearing through life with your engine running at full throttle all the time, burning up your motor, and stripping your gears. One day, all the warning lights start flashing on your dashboard, telling you to slow down, you're in trouble. But you ignore it. You keep on going, and push the override button. In fact, you don't just push it, you stand on it. When you ignore all the warning signs like that, you start to self-destruct."

Though he didn't strike me as a grease-under-the-fingernails kind of guy, Dr. Fricke gave me another automotive analogy. During a session in which I was blaming myself for not being able to take the pace at L&B, for being weaker than other people, he observed, "Some people are Mack trucks, and some Lamborghinis. Mack trucks are heavy-duty vehicles; you can run them hard every day, and they just keep on going. You can run a Lamborghini hard and fast, too, but it's a finely calibrated piece of equipment. After you race a Lamborghini, you have to put in the shop and give it a tune-up.

"A Mack truck's not better than a Lamborghini. Or vice versa. But it's important to know which kind of vehicle you're dealing with. Which one would you say you are?"

I did not fail the quiz.

In another early session Dr. Fricke came up with an image that has remained painted in watercolors on my inward eyes ever since. "Ann Keiffer, when you get to the place where you can just sit on a rock in the sun, do nothing, *and still feel good about yourself,* you will have arrived."

Implicit in every one of those observations was an indictment of my glossified Ann. I was beginning to see the gulf between the person I was and the one I thought I should be. But the Old-Ann was so much to give up. Who would I be if not her? My fear was *nothing.*

During this time, while I was reading a library book, I came across a statement that went something like this: "What makes you suicidal is trying to function as if you feel normal and strong, when in fact you feel awful." Slowly I began to realize what any rational person could have told me months earlier: The *real* Ann was worn out and needed to go on a sabbatical from her work. Perhaps she might need to give it up completely.

But that would mean I'd be *nothing!*

I was torn by a conflict that hit with the force of a hurricane slamming into a tiny island. Which was it to be? Give up everything or carry on?

———

For me, depression had been a double whammy. First, I had been flattened by the deadening despair of the depression itself. Second, because of the depression, I'd had to give up the job that had defined my life. Either whammy, all by itself, would have been enough to lay me low. Now, here I was considering that I might have to give up even all pretense of working.

In my tyranny of I-AMs and I-MUSTs, the MUST of working was king. I AM what I produce; Duke had me convinced of that. If I quit free-lancing, I'd be admitting total defeat. If I couldn't handle that relatively relaxed, self-directed pace as a writer, what could I handle? I mentally smacked myself around for being weak, or possibly lazy. I was afraid if I took down my free-lancing shingle, I'd lose all courage and never work again.

If ever there was anything I needed to talk to Dr. Fricke about, this was it. We'd already discussed the driven and draining way I'd continued to try to work since leaving L&B. Now I sat in his office and told him I thought it was over. I didn't feel I could write another word. I'd been dredging drops of creativity out of a dry well for eight months, and I was used up. I didn't have the will or the energy to go through the motions any longer. And I asked him point-blank what I should do. Did he think I should step back from work for awhile?

When I asked that specific question, "What should I do?" an "Aha!" slowly spread across Dr. Fricke's face. Then, after an almost imperceptible pause, he threw me such a curve ball I could have hit it from the dugout. He laughed and said, "Boy, you sure do make it enticing to tell you what to do! And I'll bet you don't even know you're doing it, or how good you are at it.

"Even though I know better, I'm actually tempted to give you answers. If you're this good at getting people to tell you what to do, it makes me think you've had some practice. It makes me think maybe you've been trying to get answers from other people all your life. What do you think?"

My eyebrows pulled together, and I smiled a little, out of embarrassment and confusion. Could it be true? I'd never thought of myself that way, but I had the uneasy feeling there might be as much as a lifetime of truth in what he'd observed. It was an idea that deserved close attention.

"I'm not going to tell you whether or not you should stop working," Dr. Fricke went on. "We can talk about it, but it's your decision.

"I know you'd do *anything* anyone told you to do in order to get well. But that's not the way it works here.

"This is *your* therapy. These are *your* sessions. *You* are going to decide what we should talk about. *You* are going to decide what to work on next. You'll even be in charge of telling me when your therapy is finished, when you think you're so well you don't need to come back here any more.

"I don't have answers for you. You have your own answers. I'm just here to listen, comment, and give you new ways to look at things once in awhile.

"Can you imagine how burned out I'd be if I thought I was responsible for healing my clients? I don't heal my clients. People always heal themselves.

"And by the way, let's forget this Dr. Fricke stuff. Call me Al."

Hmmmmm. For all these months I'd been so sure I wanted to figure things out for myself, to learn to swim on my own. Now I felt like I'd just been thrown in the water and was dropping like a stone.

Little did I know. At that moment I had only half an

inkling just how much Al's new you're-in-charge policy was going to press me. How it was going to yank my chain. How it was going to, almost literally, frustrate me into getting well. How it was going to make me want to bop Al repeatedly with one of his very own foam rubber boffing sticks.

————

Okay, so Dr. Fricke, Al, was not going to help me decide whether I should quit working. All through those first weeks, he *had* expressed incredulity when I talked about wanting to go back to L&B someday. Like Larry, he wondered why in the world I had the desire to subject myself to the stresses, deadlines, and corporate politics again. Whatever was driving me in that direction was something we *could* talk about. But he wasn't going to offer so much as an opinion about whether I should stop working.

For months I'd been so turned inward I felt like a corkscrew. But this decision over whether or not to continue working forced me to go inward in a new way. It forced me to look more deeply at what had happened, who I was, and what I really needed.

The booming voice of my armored-tank self was commanding me to grind on, of course, no matter what. I'd lost the best job in the whole wide world. Surely I wasn't going to give up what little I had left in the way of self-esteem by quitting free-lancing, too. But I simply could not grind on. One day I finally realized that the two sides of myself I had met earlier, Duke and Valentine, might have something to say about this:

I go into a sickroom. Valentine is lying on a narrow bed. Her face is gray; she seems near death and can barely speak. I call Duke to come into her room. Valentine brightens a little at his arrival. I ask Duke to bring her some tea and toast on a tray. Duke comes back with the tray and stands beside Valentine's bed. "Help her," I urge. After a few seconds, he puts the tray down and pours a cup of tea. Then, disgusted, he abruptly dumps the tea on Valentine! I order Duke to leave, to stay away from Valentine until he can be accepting and loving. He leaves. I pour another cup of tea, lift Valentine's head, and hold the cup to her lips so she can drink.

I was shocked. This Duke was the aspect of myself I had been letting rule my life? By being a slave to my masculine values, I was killing my own inner feminine.

Finally, on my own, I did what I should have done eight months before. I quit work. At least I quit my free-lancing business. I promised myself I would not attempt to write again until my creative well was full once more, until a new assignment actually sounded like fun. I didn't know if that would be in a month or six months or never.

Letting go of I-MUST-WORK felt like jumping out of an airplane without a parachute. Even after I'd jumped, the Old-Ann kicked and screamed and refused to be thwarted. Almost as soon as I'd decided to quit free-lancing, she started nagging me to *do something* else. If I wasn't going to free-lance, I should at least get some kind of undemanding part-time job. (That way, I'd be doing something that justified my existence and brought in some money.)

I was pathetic. I was afraid not to work. I looked morosely through the want ads and made myself interview for a sales position at a local department store. As soon as I'd answered the interviewer's question about what my salary had been on my last job and the nature of my responsibilities, I was given a puzzled look and a hasty thank-you-very-much-but-no-thanks-and-good-bye. The interviewer had more sense than I did.

When was I going to get it? When was I going to give it up and get on with the business of getting well? Larry shook his head over me. My friends shook their heads over me. My head was almost too hard to shake.

Finally, I could see there was no other choice. I had to give in to the tired and broken part of me. About nine months too late, I gave up working. I told Larry I would not work again for as long as it was going to take to get well. I was too exhausted to do anything else. Still, it was so hard to leave that MUST behind. I entered unemployment with the halting hesitancy I would have used walking naked into a glacier-fed lake.

Sick. Unemployed. Depressed. "Larry," I'd say, "Are you sure I'm still getting better and better every day?" His answer was, "Yes."

———

What does a person do with an unstructured day? I had no idea. I didn't have a hobby. I lived in a condo with only a few clay pots as my garden. I didn't paint. I didn't sew. I didn't play the piano. I wasn't a cleaning fanatic. I didn't have a houseful of little children to love and tend and feed.

What does a person do with approximately fifteen empty hours that come around like clockwork in every twenty-four? To most people, fifteen empty hours may sound like heaven; to me, it was hell. If that sounds demented, it was. But I'd been living life according to my crazed game plan for years; now I was in culture shock — the culture of leisure, downtime, and healing was indeed foreign territory to me.

I'd wake up in the morning with the whole empty day stretching out in front of me. *You have to do something, do something do something with all this time! Hurry up! Fill it up!*, my mind clamored. I'd be frantic to do . . . what? I had to feel my way into each big blank day because I didn't know how to relax or just "be."

I was confused. And still so sluggish and draggy, draggy tired. Still so in need of answers. But my mind was like a collector's ball of string; I couldn't see where to get hold of an end piece so I could start to unwind it.

Each week, with Al, I would discuss what was happening, but he wouldn't tell me what to do. I was so frustrated I went away from each of our sessions wanting to Bop! Bop! Bop! him with those "boffing sticks" in his office. It's not that he wasn't wonderful; he was accessible, active, and supportive in every way. I just couldn't get him to give me answers — which was doubly upsetting because I didn't even know the questions yet!

In addition to not giving me answers, Al made another very major contribution toward my recovery. One afternoon in March, he was coming in from his lunchtime walk around the block just as I was arriving for my appointment. He unlocked the door of the office and stood there grinning, waiting for me, then only watching.

A few minutes later, after we'd settled into our chairs in his office, Al said, "I watched you as you were getting out of the car and walking in, and I think you may be overmedicated. Your movements are slow. Your speech is slow, too. It's not my place to prescribe, but I think you might want to consider tapering off your antidepressants."

I was shocked. At that point the antidepressants seemed an essential part of my existence. I was afraid if I stopped taking them, I'd slip right back into the terror of not sleeping and not eating again. I told Al that and said I just didn't see how I could stop.

Al said, "It's up to you. But I think the antidepressants may be adding to how fatigued you've been feeling.

"I see patients at the Veterans Administration Hospital twice a week. Sometimes getting them *off* medication is just as important as getting them on. Friends and relatives come in and say, 'Oh, Charlie seems so much better this week!' and all that's happened is we've taken him off his medication. Do what you think is best. I'm just telling you what I observed."

I knew, Larry knew, everyone who knew me, knew: I talked so slowly my voice sounded like a bad recording; I was tired all the time and moved only in slow motion. If getting off the antidepressants would help all that, maybe I should give them up. Besides, it had always bothered me that Dr. Wong had automatically raised my dosage each time I reported feeling down, time after time. Maybe Al was right.

I talked with Dr. Wong about getting off my medication, and he instructed me on how to taper off gradually. Then I let go of another lifeline and slowly stopped my antidepressants. While my energy did not return in a rush, I did feel some degree of physical relief as I began to taper off — less weighed-down, less mind-bogged, less leaden-tongued.

Several weeks later I called Dulcie and told her, "I'm almost afraid to say this out loud, but I think I am actually getting better."

What I said was greeted by silence because Dulcie left

the phone. When she came back on a few seconds later, she was sniffling, and her words were tremulous with tears. "I didn't realize how much I'd missed you," she said. "It feels like you've been away for so long, and now your voice sounds like you're coming back."

I *was* coming back. I was getting better and better every day. Slowly, but very, very surely.

9

Inching
Along the
Tightrope

About the same time I started seeing Al — partly because I'd read that exercise is a spirit-lifter for people who are depressed, but mainly because it got me out of the house two mornings a week — I decided to try something new. I joined a low-impact aerobics class at the Y. In my case that meant very low impact because moving my arms and legs felt like trying to sling wet sandbags. I was surprised to find that it did feel good to get my blood pumping.

Around the same time I also enrolled in a movement class at a Bay area school of psychology offering innovative community classes in addition to its degree programs. Our class there was led by a woman who was both a marriage/family therapist and a movement therapist.

I've always loved to dance, but this was dancing with a

new dimension. The purpose of the class was to give us a kinesthetic way to learn about ourselves and how we interact with the world. During class, we moved to an eclectic mix of music and drum rhythms. We experimented with dancing mad-sad-happy-afraid, with acting out different aspects of ourselves as we played around with scarves or capes or exotic hats, with mirroring each other's movements to see what we could learn. And we were asked to keep a record of our experiences. For me, the issue of masculine and feminine values arose as a primary focus.

Excerpts from My Movement Class Notebook

Class #1:

My movement class started tonight. We worked with masculine and feminine issues in the realm of movement. I felt at home with the masculine, aggressive side, which we labeled "Making It Happen." I valued that side of myself. But I didn't feel comfortable with the feminine, accepting side; I felt I should just lie down and be totally passive to indicate acceptance. And that felt wimpy. All the way home from class I tried to think of a phrase to fit the feminine side that would make me feel good about it, something as valuable as "Making It Happen." I came up with "Being Moved By Inspiration."

I also realized that you can't really "make it happen" without first having that infinitesimal flash of "being moved by inspiration." Life is always an interplay between the two. Maybe the hard part is not getting stuck in either mode, but letting them flow.

Class #2:

I noticed how small and quiet my movements were tonight. It seemed indicative of my real physical and emotional state of being right now. I was filled with compassion for myself because of the difficult journey I've been on these last months. I've been trying to act normal, pretend nothing's happened, carry on doing normal activities. But, in fact, I've come through a tremendous ordeal and should be gentle with myself. Healing is still going on.

Class #3:

Today was a hard day for letting myself be moved by inspiration or for letting it be. I felt like I was constantly making something happen. I think I may have wanted to go to the beach, or lie on my back and look at the sky, or climb to a high place and watch the world go by. But I didn't.

Class #4:

Driving to class, I noticed how depressed I feel. I don't have a purpose in life. "Being" is not enough. When I had a job, I knew why I should get up in the morning. I had something exciting and challenging to do. Now I don't.

I don't want to fill my days with meaningless pastimes. Or is this my learning experience, to learn to enjoy the basics of life — cooking, reading, walking, visiting friends? It doesn't sound so bad; it's just that I think I should be doing something else. What is the purpose in this?

————

Perhaps those few entries in the movement class note-book were the catalyst that led to the dramatic break-through that followed. Because I could not get any answers from Al, I was driven further and further inward. Finally one morning in April, I picked up my pen and a pad of paper I kept beside the bed and began writing.

I don't know why I began writing my thoughts that particular morning, except to fill some time in an otherwise empty day, or maybe to release some of the anxiety I was feeling about not knowing where I was going in my life. But as I wrote, I was surprised to discover that it brought me back to center, to some kind of still point in myself.

I began to keep a journal — not on purpose in the beginning. But, over time, writing about what I was feeling became an integral part of my life. I called the process "sorting," as in sorting my thoughts, and sometimes I'd write for as long as two hours at a time. I didn't write in my journal every day. But whenever I was upset, feeling sad or confused, or at odds with myself, I wrote and wrote and wrote until I came to some sense of closure about the problem.

Writing in my journal clarified my thinking, gave me insights, helped calm me down, allowed me to get some kind of handle on whatever was happening. I was amazed at how much I could teach myself, at all the inner wisdom I scratched and blobbed onto ordinary lined yellow tablets with my ballpoint pen day after day. Keeping that journal became an important tool for my recovery.

One night not long after that, I experienced a pro-found moment of insight. Just as I was drifting into the echoing darkness between wakefulness and sleep, something that looked like a diamond-laser-star flashed into my mind's eye. Suddenly that diamond-star pierced the blackness of my inner night sky, sending down a laser beam. In the next instant that laser beam struck me in the solar plexus, surging up and down my body like fifteen hundred volts of electricity.

I cannot explain what happened that night. I know only that diamond-laser-star vision burst forth in my mind's eye unbidden. And while the vision existed wholly within my psyche, the laser strike was a very real physical experience, with mysterious energy vibrating for several miraculous minutes in my body. While I cannot explain it, I knew this experience was a promise of healing. I might not be well right then, or even tomorrow, but I knew with certainty that I could become whole again. Out of depression came the Magnificently Creative Life Force for which I had been searching.

All through April and for the next few months, I wrote in my journal nearly every day, and my ongoing healing process was apparent in everything I wrote. Even when I was struggling, going up and down with depression, I was making discoveries. Instead of being bound in by glossified-but-killing rules, I was uncovering a more authentic way to live, developing the courage to become an individual, someone who could actually *respond* to life.

Excerpts from My Personal Journal:

April 16, 1984:
I don't want to go to aerobics today. It's just one more make-work, fill-up-your-time attempt to escape from myself and my predicament.

All day Friday I felt like I was trying to escape from myself. I was scared that I had nothing to do, panicked at hours ahead with nothing to engage me. I was running away, hurrying to fill up my time so I wouldn't have to feel the emptiness.

What's so bad about being with myself? First, it's boring because I don't have interests or hobbies. Second, I'm uncomfortable just "being." My attention span for daydreaming or watching the birds or contemplation is only a few minutes . . . then I feel I've got to do something constructive.

What in the world has really happened to me? What is a mental or emotional or nervous breakdown? At Spectrum they said it was a "stress reaction" and an "organic chemical imbalance." But that doesn't explain what happened to me.

I feel I had a personality or identity or a life held together with gum, rubber bands, and what other people thought of me. In order to keep functioning or working, I had to build this house of cards higher and higher, trying harder and harder to please. There was a period of time when I felt good about myself, sassy and unafraid to say what I thought. But somewhere along the way, something went wrong. I kept trying to bolster the house of cards, but the gum wasn't holding.

I started feeling the joy had gone out of my job. It was all give and no take. I wasn't receiving joy or satisfaction from the work I was doing. I felt empty, with no reserves, no creative energy. But I still kept trying, wanting to please. The house of cards was really shaky. Then one day the whole structure came tumbling down.

Now, with no job, I don't know who I am. I don't even have my house of cards to live in. I'm vulnerable on every side, alone, exposed, raw, without purpose or direction, having to start my life again. And still I don't have a better plan. Al Fricke keeps pointing out that I'm trying to rebuild the same old house of cards again.

So what am I to do? Where do I begin? Al would probably say I begin by being here now. I hate being here now. I hate experiencing my panic, fear, anger, hopelessness. I'm sick of feeling bad and incapacitated. I'm sick of feeling like an invalid who can't handle the rigors of life. I feel so turned in on my own navel I could spit. If turning inward gave me any positive direction, it might be worthwhile. But I don't think all this writing and thinking has done me very much good. What do I know now — how am I any better off than months ago?

I don't want to kill myself now. I've discovered some brief moments of happiness in my movement class. I have had a number of good days where I feel life is changing for the better. I'm crying less often. I'm almost off my medication. I've been able to sleep through the night without medication. I've been able to spend some days successfully entertaining myself.

But the problem is, I feel bad right now. Not up. Not sure it will all turn out. Not sure I'll work again. Not confident. Not successful. And I'm so impatient. I want to be better right now, to jump back in the mainstream of life, to forget myself and everything that's happened to me. To play and work with abandon.

I know my emotions are my responsibility; maybe the problem is I keep trying to change them — from negative to positive, from fear to confidence. It's damn hard work always pushing and prodding myself to feel different, change my moods. I wonder what would happen if I stopped resisting and just let myself feel negative or fearful or hopeless? I'd never get out of it. I'd be totally incapacitated by my down side.

I am not inner-directed. I want answers and guidance from outside myself. I don't trust that I have the answers. Becoming inner-directed is a key issue in my recovery.

April 18, 1984:
In a way I feel like I'm walking a tightrope. I'm balancing on the rope, trying to set one foot carefully in front of the other in healing myself. When I start comparing my life to other people's lives, when I start looking back at the great job I used to have or looking ahead at how I'm ever going to get back to work again, I lose my balance. I teeter on the rope. I lose my direction and my own first fragile indications that I'm doing what is right for myself, that life is going to turn out. When I lose my focus and concentration, I get afraid I'm not doing this right. I start thinking I don't even want to be on this tightrope; I don't want to deal with an emotional breakdown and the chaos it caused in my life.

The only thing I can do is hold out my umbrella or balancing pole and concentrate on getting my balance again, thinking only of how to put one foot in front of the other and of "being here now" — without comparing myself to others, without frantic attempts to escape from myself, without worrying how I'll get to the other side of the tightrope and back to work again. It feels like it's a full-time job for me to stay centered and balanced — doing what is absolutely right and necessary for me right now.

(When I told Al about my tightrope image, he observed that at first it would seem like a very thin wire, but as time went on I'd find it was actually a two-by-four, and finally a bridge.)

April 23, 1984:
What have I learned from this breakdown and recovery period?

I've learned that I don't know much about pacing myself. I've always tried to prove myself by going all out in the things that matter to me — even when it's been to my own detriment. I put goals in front of myself without regard for what's going on in my life. I have a difficult time being appropriate with myself.

I've learned that I'm out of touch with my own warning signals, intuition, instincts. My body gave me all kinds of signals that I was in trouble, but I didn't get the significance of what it was saying. If my body is disturbed or out of whack in any way, I probably need to examine emotions I haven't been expressing or look to see what I need to do to better take care of myself.

I've learned that I didn't put my own needs first. I made other people and the ad agency more important than my health and well-being. I see now that I need to stay in touch with what my needs are — all the time — and make it a priority to take care of myself first. I'm no good to anyone else if I don't take care of myself.

I've learned that I have been an outer-directed person, and that I need to learn to become an inner-directed person. Instead of searching for answers from other people, I need to discover my own opinion, my own advice to myself, my own way. And I need to take an assertive stand on what I discover to be true for myself.

I've learned that this depression went on — in fact, became worse — the more I tried to get back to "normal" life. What was required for resolution and healing was a willingness to spend time doing some solitary soul-searching. I learned that my thoughts and feelings crystallized in a way that began to heal me when I spent time alone, writing to sort out what was going on in my mind.

I learned that escaping into part-time jobs or good works or friends or housework was counter-productive toward my real need — the need to experience being alone so I could sort out the chaos in my inner (and outer) life in a positive way.

I learned that my creative energy could be misused and abused, that it could go underground and "disappear," leaving me as dead as a stone, without hope, passion, or interest in anyone or anything. But I also learned that energy wasn't gone forever; it just wasn't accessible for a long time. I've learned that at times I want to be alone.

I've learned that my therapy wasn't limited to work in Al's office. I had to do a lot of work on my own on the outside. That was very difficult, because I wanted Al to tell me what to do, give me assignments, answers. I felt frantic, thinking I had to rely on myself. Getting easy answers wouldn't have helped me in the long run, though. I needed tools for living. I needed to learn I could rely on myself to figure things out and take a course of action.

April 25, 1984:
In the last two weeks I've suddenly felt the lifting of this nine-month-long suicidal depression, but I'm almost afraid to rejoice. It feels like it may come back to overtake me. I don't trust that I'm cured. I begin to worry about the future, instead of living one day at a time . . . I almost feel a little nostalgic remorse for the former days of wrestling with depression — at least I knew what my life was about then. Now what?

I'll say it to myself again: I have to respect the life-loving little kid in me, play with people, get a kick out of whatever I'm doing. I don't work or do household jobs or exercise to escape from myself; I do these things to enjoy myself, to delve into the joy of living. Whatever I do, I do for the satisfaction and joy it will bring me and others by association!

Stay on that tightrope; put one foot in front of the other, maintain your balance. The ups and downs and distractions are there, but you can take them in stride if you focus on the moment now.

(At about this time, I received a call from a prospective client, and I *wanted* to take the job. After two months off, I was ready to free-lance — with a new attitude toward work, I hoped.)

April 26, 1984:
I was so high after the meeting with my clients, I ran at a hectic pace until after 10:00 p.m. I felt as if I'd never been sick, as if I could go back to work full-time, as if I could lick the world. Then, like gravity, my body brought me back down to earth . . . I'm feeling tired and wasted

and down in my spirits. It's hard not to let this invalidate my positive movement. Part of me thinks I'm going to be miserable forever. It's hard to take it in stride as the next step in my recovery.

Al gave me the example of a kid who's recovering from a broken leg. The kid can't run and play rough-and-tumble right away because his muscles have atrophied from being in a cast. He has to pace his exercise and, if the leg hurts, he knows he's one too far. Well, I've gone too far.

I need to acknowledge that full recovery takes time. I'm beginning to recover. I'm making real progress. Though I may have setbacks from time to time as I learn to pace myself better.

It is not realistic to think I'll always feel great, enthusiastic, and positive. Nobody does. Life has a natural rhythm of ups and downs. It's just that I want so much to be all the way better — I'm in such a hurry — that I'm afraid of any downward turn in my spirits. I resist it instead of taking it in stride and experiencing it fully, then letting it go, completely.

I feel bad right now . . . but, hey, wait a minute, here's a new thought: Feeling bad isn't necessarily permanent. I don't know what I will feel in the next instant or tomorrow!

May 1, 1984:

I feel like I'm sliding back into depression. I've been thinking I'm tense because I'm trying to protect myself, but it's probably more accurate to say I've been trying to "gear up" to face work and problems and be "up" for my clients. I feel what a toll that attitude is taking on my *physical and emotional well-being. Once again, I'm trying to pretend things are normal, that I can go on with life as usual. It's not working!*

I want so much to be better. I'm tired of walking, being careful, paying attention to myself. I want to rush ahead, live normally, be in on the action, be in the fast lane. Instead, here I am, balancing on a tightrope, needing to put one foot very slowly in front of the other, to focus on doing only and exactly what I need to do to keep my balance. It's hard, painstaking, individual work.

June 30, 1984:

During the last couple of weeks I've felt tired, uncreative, driven, and unhappy — not to mention sick. Here's what I have to say to me:

Breaks! *No project, appointment, deadline, or errand is so pressing you can't take time to watch the birds, have a cup of tea, go for a walk, or lie in the sun for a few minutes and look at the trees. When you take breaks, you feel better and your creativity flows more freely — so the finished product is better.*

Watch your goal orientation! *It's more important to feel happy, creative, and satisfied with what you're doing than to finish it by such and such a time. You gain nothing by pushing.*

Choose your jobs carefully! *There's plenty of work. Accept the projects you'll enjoy, ones you really have time for. You're looking for satisfaction, not money or quantity. Limit your workload.*

Eat right! *Take time to fix good food and take your time eating it. Slow down.*

Don't forget to exercise! *A walk, aerobics at*

home, anything that gets your heart pumping and your muscles working.

November 23, 1984:
I don't know what's going on. I've got an ocean of tears behind my eyes. I'm blue, low key.

Hey! I think that's what "blue" means to me! If I'm not in high spirits, I think I'm depressed. Yes, yes, yes!

You know what? I'm not really depressed; I just want to be quiet and warm and unhurried today. I don't want to do anything for anyone, to perform. I need downtime. My body's saying, "I want to lie down and rest." So that's what I'm going to do.

———

I've included journal excerpts from April through November to illustrate that changing my ways was grueling, painstaking, arduous work. Coming to terms with myself and my new lifestyle required daily practice — and a willingness to keep surrendering over and over to reality and the truth.

By June of 1984, I felt excited about having my depression lift. I was still physically fragile and tired, but emotionally, I felt much better. And I knew I did not need to see Al any longer.

At the end of what Al and I both knew was my last session, I said good-bye, got my car keys out of my purse, and headed for the door. But as I was walking away, I realized something was missing. I turned and looked at Al. "Is it okay for a person to hug her therapist?" I asked. We hugged mightily, breaking into one last good laugh together. Then I said good-bye again . . . and wanted only to bop Al a little. I was very, very grateful.

It wasn't the end of my journey. But almost.

———

By late spring of 1984, my depression was over. I felt I had beaten my Dark Angel, and I was ready to run to the top of a mountain just so I could shout hosannas from the peak!

My spirits were singing with life again. At last, at long last, my enthusiasm for everyday pleasures — eating, reading, talking, working, making love, cooking, walking — had reawakened. I felt as if I had been raised from the dead.

What a blessing! What a miracle! I was grateful for the wisdom I had gained from my depression. I felt I now understood the importance of pacing myself and looking inward for answers. And I believed I was living in a way that was consistent with these new insights.

But my body still held a riddle of mysteries.

Though I had gotten better and better every day in so many ways — just as Larry had predicted — I still had recurring problems with insomnia, chills, a foggy memory, and poor concentration. And I was always, always fatigued. Compared with what I'd just been through, though, these symptoms seemed only about as troublesome as a bad summer cold. So that spring I resumed my work, my friendships, and what I thought was a not-too-hectic normal life.

Still, I was concerned that the symptoms which had seemed to herald my depression were continuing to hang on even after the depression had lifted. To my credit, I didn't shrug off my body's warning signs without a second thought this time. When the yearly opportunity to switch medical plans rolled around, we left Spectrum and chose coverage that would allow us to choose any doctor we wished. Within a few weeks I scouted out an M.D. who was both a good detective and interested in taking on my case. However, I passed my physical and every lab test she could order. No matter how often we put our heads together over my persistent health problems, we could not seem to find a clinical cause or a magic pill that would make me well.

When my doctor wasn't able to implicate a specific disease or germ as the cause of my ills, I began to believe I might be one of those people sometimes referred to in a half-whisper as "delicate." The word made me think of consumptives and invalids of Victorian days. Though I didn't relish this image of myself — in a swoon on a green velvet divan, overcome by an attack of the vapors — I decided there was little I could do but accept my physical limitations, respect them, and learn to work around them.

For the next two years I worked hard at taking good care of myself. I tried to remember to pace myself between errands, work, and household tasks — never taking on too much. I hung a sign over my computer that read, "The show need not go on . . . the mail need not go through." Occasionally, I even let the bathrooms go dirty.

But I was never quite well.

Was my life still calling out to me to change? It was not a question I asked myself then. It is a question I ask myself now. I am reminded of therapist Judith Duerk's words:

> If a woman cannot let herself hear her own needs, but continues to adhere fearfully to a lifestyle that denies her inner growth and deepening, the voice of the Self may manifest in physical illness as the only possible way to force her to take time to be with herself.[5]

In late November of 1985, I was unexpectedly struck down by physical pain. You may understand the nature of this pain if I tell you it was as if I had just given birth — my labia felt slashed, scalded, and brutally, achingly swollen. But I had no pretty little baby to show for my anguish.

Between 1986 and 1988, this pain drove me to specialists of every stripe and hue — gynecologists, internists, dermatologists, dermapathologists, allergists, Chinese acupuncturists, urologists, and many more. During those two years, I went down more blind alleys than a stray cat with glaucoma. Not one doctor had ever seen a problem like this. Oh, they ventured hypotheses, tested, pulled all sorts of pharmaceutical rabbits out of hats. But ultimately, they all ended up shaking their heads, becoming vaguely distant in their professional guilt over not being able to do anything to ease my misery.

The more these doctors failed, the harder I had to work to master the feat of living at the intersection of expectancy and stasis. I felt like a gymnast suspended high in midair, quivering from the effort of practicing the stationary iron cross on free-swinging rings. In one hand, I grasped passionate hope for better physical health. With the other hand, I seized reality — the absolute necessity of accepting my health exactly as it was. There, between the two extremes, I tried to hold the tension and live my life.

From my vantage point on the rings, I could see it wasn't going to be possible to put my fate in the hands of a doctor; nobody wanted responsibility for my fate. So even while I continued to follow leads to new specialists, I knew I had to be responsible for my own health care. After all, nobody else had as much incentive to solve my problem as I did; nobody else was sitting on the problem every day.

While I tried to resign myself to living with pain as real and present as a razor blade tearing inflamed flesh, I was always on the lookout for information or any clue that might help me end the agony. I free-lanced for my advertising clients as usual, but I also cross-examined biochemists and read obscure medical papers. I chatted with friends at casual dinner parties — and became a guinea pig for a research clinic. I peeled potatoes for dinner and did the laundry — and ran experiments eliminating possible culprits: foods, fabric softeners, soaps, toilet paper. (Hadn't I been through all this once before?)

I was so good at my double life, Dulcie said I ought to wear a black armband when I was hurting — so my friends would never forget the misery I was in. And I *was* in misery. I downed aspirin by threes, every six hours. I tried ice bags, heating pads, first-aid creams, and sitz baths on my battered bottom, always hoping for relief that never came. Day after day, I sat on that pain, stood with that pain, walked with it, slept with it. I hurt. Oh, how I hurt.

Many nights I lay in Larry's arms, weeping — because on most days my labia were so painful we could not make love. We improvised. We were very careful. Larry was always accepting and tender, but it made me so sad. I didn't even feel like a woman any more. My pain and the passion to be free of it became the warp in the woof of all my days.

Finally, in the spring of 1988, I ended up in what I considered the office of last resort. I had an appointment with Dr. Phyllis Saifer, a clinical ecologist/allergist whose specialty seemed to be unsolved mysteries of the chronically ill — poor souls so bad off it seemed possible they might be allergic to air or water or life itself. Two times I had made and cancelled appointments with Dr. Saifer, each time refusing to admit I was *that* bad off. But finally there seemed nowhere else left to go.

So there I was one bright day in April, sitting on a molded plastic chair in Dr. Saifer's bare, spare waiting room, right next to an industrial-size air purifier and a sign that read: *Please! No scented soaps, lotions, perfumes, deodorants, or hairspray. Many of our patients are sensitive to these products.*

Looking around for a distraction, I got up to browse the bulletin board and found it posted with ads for organic grooming supplies and newspaper clippings about people so environmentally ill they'd had to move far from civilization and live in sod houses lined with Reynolds Wrap. Just what I was afraid of. I was sure this doctor was going to tell me the only way I was going to get well was to shave my head instead of my legs, eliminate all foods except seaweed and soybeans, and go live in a cave a thousand miles from the dead center of nowhere.

When the receptionist called my name and pointed me into this end-of-the-line doctor's office, I expected to see gray cement block walls and a gray, morose doctor. Instead, the walls were painted creamy white, and the bare vinyl-tiled floor was polished to a dazzle. Built-in shelves displayed books, paintings, silk flowers, and rows of family-and-friends photos as warm as the sunshine that was pouring into the room like a benediction.

In this office there was no metal or wood barricade of a desk for a doctor to hide behind. A glass pedestal table, glinting green all the way around its elegant beveled edges, was angled jauntily across one corner of the room. As I walked in, Dr. Saifer stood up from behind her see-through desk and came to greet me at the door.

Petite, probably in her late fifties, Dr. Saifer was wearing a dress of rich, burnished hues, accented by an abstract, handcrafted pin. Her black hair, shot with strands of pewter, was drawn loosely back in a bun. Holding my chart snugged up under her left arm, she smiled warmly, introduced herself, and reached out with her right hand to touch my arm as she welcomed me in. This was not at all what I'd expected. She was all color, intensity, and compassion, this Dr. Saifer . . . and very, very deep in the eyes.

As she was taking my medical history, Dr. Saifer would lift her gaze to the ceiling occasionally and ask reflectively, "What could make a woman so sick?" Yes, what *could* make a woman so sick?, I wondered, too.

I noticed that Dr. Saifer was also nodding her head, yes, in response to my answers to certain questions. Into that small gesture I read the possibility that my grab bag of symptoms might actually be making some kind of logical sense to her. As the interview continued, I realized she was asking me more and more questions about my depression, a subject which, initially, I had mentioned only in passing.

After almost an hour of verbal probing, Dr. Saifer pushed back her chair and walked around the side of her glass desk to do some physical probing. Pressing her fingertips gently all around my throat, she smiled and said she had a hunch.

A week later, the lab tests verified it: I had an autoimmune disorder called Hashimoto's thyroiditis. Dr. Saifer said she didn't understand how thyroiditis might be causing my most recent pain, but treating the thyroid problem was the place to start.

In lay terms, the thyroiditis diagnosis meant that my immune system had turned on me, going on full-tilt red alert. For some reason my immune system now viewed my thyroid gland and the thyroxin it produces as enemies and was developing antibodies to destroy them. My thyroid was swollen and inflamed, and all body systems that needed thyroxin were gradually being compromised. Somewhere along the way, I had become allergic to myself.

My list of symptoms — especially agitation and fatigue, insomnia, poor short-term memory and concentration, and a history of skin and gastrointestinal allergies — read like the doctor's manual on Hashimoto's thyroiditis. And when Dr. Saifer explained the emotional aspects of the disease, I sat there dumbfounded . . .

The psychiatric symptoms associated with the disease include . . . are you ready for this? . . . *clinical depression.*

After recommending I read Bernie Siegel's book *Love, Medicine & Miracles* and instructing me to make an appointment with a colleague of hers, a respected endocrinologist in San Francisco, Dr. Saifer sent me home with everything I could ever have wanted to know, including a reprint of a research paper that detailed the psychiatric manifestations of Hashimoto's thyroiditis. As I read the paper, the last five years of my life tumbled jingling and flashing into place like shiny, new coins pouring through a coin-sorter.

Yes, yes, yes! Five years after my depression, the "Gordian Knot of *Why?*" was beginning to unravel. Beyond my mysterious chemical imbalance, there had been a very specific physical component in my depression. It had never, ever been all-in-my-head. What I had needed was thyroid hormone replacement therapy.

When my endocrinologist took my medical history, he pointed out that, while no one realized it then, my father also suffered from disorders which are now classified as autoimmune problems. What compassion I felt for my dad. It now seemed possible I had, in a way, inherited my depression right along with my autoimmune disorder.

Through my reading I also learned that while the disease affects men, women, and children, it is most common in women between the ages of thirty and fifty.[6] I was thirty-eight at the time my symptoms, including depression, first began to appear.

Given my textbook list of symptoms, why hadn't one

of my many doctors picked up on the correct diagnosis? While I had been given thyroid function tests several times, I had never been given a complete endocrine workup. On standard thyroid function tests, my scores always came up low-normal. Nothing to worry about. However, my endocrinologist's complete workup gave a clearer picture: My thyroid was not functioning at all on its own; it was being flogged into functioning by my pituitary gland. And my antibodies to thyroxin were high.

As one doctor told me, "Thyroiditis is insidious and insidiously deceptive." He said in medical school the axiom was: Thyroiditis is the diagnosis you'll miss in your own spouse. I believe it.

As soon as the results of my endocrine work-up came back from the lab, I was put on thyroid replacement hormone therapy. The good news was I experienced gradual improvement in some of my physical symptoms during that first year, including some improvement in my paralyzing fatigue. The bad news was there was no improvement in the pain that had driven me back to the doctors in the first place.

Another blind alley. It seemed there was no escape from this pain. But, I reminded myself, two years before I had thought there was no escape from depression, either. Relief had come . . . but only after I had done the arduous work of mining its depths for meaning. Somehow this unrelenting physical pain seemed similar. Somehow I knew my Dark Angel was still with me, standing in the dark, demanding that I search for the meaning in this experience, too.

10

Learning

To Be

*F*or years, an inner voice had been urging me to go away by myself and spend time completely alone. I don't mean I actually heard this voice; I *felt* it as a deep, silent urge that had been pulling at my bones and consciousness for years. Now, struggling with the meaning of my pain, I knew I must not, could not, say no to that voice any longer.

In April of 1988, I left on a six-day solo retreat. I drove to Big Sur and there, in the rugged mountains of the California coast, in a small cabin surrounded by towering redwoods, I descended down to the bedrock of my being, circled down and down to find the meaning in my pain.

For perhaps the first time in my life, I was truly still. During each long day of my retreat, I hardly moved from the couch that faced the window opening to the woods. I watched the sunlight slide down the trees and slowly creep away. I watched evening descend on the woods each night, and then watched the darkness itself when light was gone. I ate my meals alone in the cabin, spoke to no one, wrote in my journal, and pursued the mystery at the core of my pain.

It is difficult for me to write about the things that happened during this time of seclusion without fearing I'll sound like a religious fanatic, an aging hippie high on drugs, or a woman just plain out of touch with reality. But, I assure you, I was none of these; I have never been more in touch with reality than I was during those six days.

All my life I had believed in the existence of a transcendent power in the universe. Though I could call this power Source, or Truth, or Ultimate Reality, or Heavenly Father, or even Magnificently Creative Life Force, I usually find it easier just to say "God." So in describing my experiences at Big Sur, I will say God — knowing that the word may not have the same meaning for you that it does for me, knowing that my own definition and experience of God are fluid and expanding.

Revelation began with a candle. On the second night of my stay, I found myself rummaging through the boxes of food and supplies I'd brought with me, looking for the chunky, vanilla-scented candle I'd packed two days before. I didn't know why it was important, but, before I sat down to dinner, I needed to light that candle and place it on the table.

As darkness fell, the flame of that candle became the symbol for an insight so basic I wanted to wrap arms around it and hold it to me forever. Just as a magnifying glass can set paper aflame by focusing a few seconds of sunlight, I wanted to focus the intensity of that candle's incandescence and burn it into my memory. Find the words, I thought, write it down. In my journal I wrote this poem, "Breath of God":

"Breathe on me, Breath of God.
Fill me with life anew.
That I may love what Thou dost love,
And do what Thou wouldst do."

Alone, sitting in front of windows,
Watching the redwoods
In Big Sur
Where I'd come to search for God,
This old hymn became my prayer,
My inner song,
My mantra,
My constant thought.

Old dusty breath forced
Up out of my lungs,
Finding remnants of the voice
I used to have,
I sang the words aloud,
Sang them in my head,
Sang them in my heart,
Sang them in my soul,
Took them with me wherever I went.

At dinner
In the cottage where I stayed,
Evening sun and shadows
Made patterns on my plate,
Dancing on food seasoned with my tears.

As I listened to my music
I begged God for a sign
One sign, any sign,
a sign to let me know
that God was here.

Then a Voice inside my head said,
"What sign did you want to see?"
My eyes fell on the flickering candle
I said, "I want that flame to go out."
The Voice said,
"Blow it out."
And I said,
"Who me?"

I scoffed at such a willful gesture,
Rejected it as totally unworthy
Of the Majestic Presence I had sought.
And I did nothing
But clear up the dishes
And wait
Until at last
I shut off the lights
And blew the candle out.
With nothing changed . . .
Especially me,
Alone in the dark.

For hours from my couch
I watched the darkness
Descending ever deeper on the woods.
Then suddenly out of
The stillness of the night,

The flicker of an idea
Caught all my attention
And lit my being
In one flash of brilliant light.

What if I was needed
To make God's presence known?
What if God needed to be
Revealed not just through miracles
But through people,
People just like me?

Immediately I got to my feet.
Searching out a match,
I made my way through the dusky cottage
And relit the candle in the kitchen.
Then consciously, willingly
In one breath
Blew it out . . .
In God's name.

It was a small thing, that flame,
So small, yet it lit my life forever.
What I'd asked for was a miracle,
Majesty, a Divine Epiphany.
And I received all three . . .
In one divinely simple
Opportunity.
Yes, breathe on me, Breath of God.
I drew God's own breath
Into my lungs
And blew my candle out.

Something was there in the darkness and the solitude, moving with me and through me.

Then, on the third night of my retreat, I came upon the vein of gold I'd hoped to find hidden in the depths of pain. How could I have missed the point? Of course . . . this pain was such a graphic symbol of a wound of the most feminine part of me. What if the feminine side of my nature was burning and aching for expression? Maybe I was trying to give birth to something feminine within myself.

If this symbology were true, I believed it might be Valentine who brought me to Big Sur — my own inner woman. Perhaps it was her voice I had been hearing all these years, urging me toward solitude and deepening. Perhaps Valentine was to be the midwife for the birth of something new in me. I remembered the suffering written on Valentine's face so many years before, her feet so broken and dirty. Now those feet seemed to signify wisdom gathered on long journeys through life. Was I suffering because I had neglected, discounted, or despised that knowing wisdom in myself?

I was more puzzled than ever. What was I to do about this revelation, this wound, this need to cherish feminine values? How strange! When I thought about it, I seemed to have no experience, information, or ideas about what the feminine actually was. How could I not know what "feminine" was? Was it something to do with nurturing? Well, give me some time, I thought, and I'd figure it out. Then my pain would go away; I was sure of it. I had three days left, and I made it my goal to solve this riddle before I had to leave for home on Friday.

Day four passed me by empty-handed. There was no revelation, no insight into this mystery of the feminine.

But on the morning of day five, I made the following entry in my journal:

> *Wretched night, ending wonderfully. I could not sleep, felt sick and tired, had a bad "burn" on my bottom and had to get up five times in the night, lots of pain. Felt very distressed — like I'd gotten nowhere on this retreat.*
>
> *Finally, sometime around 4:00 a.m., I was lying awake and remembered I could try talking directly to God. I begged again for some reassurance, some sign of God's presence with me in this pain. Again, I heard the Voice that made no sound: "Ann, what do you think all these moments — even hours — of peace have been here at Big Sur?"*
>
> *I said, "That was Your presence?"*
>
> *The Voice said, "When have you ever once felt like that before?"*
>
> *That made me laugh because it was so true. I think it's true I need to learn to practice peace. ·Maybe that's part of what I need to learn about feminine values. It's beginning to seem that my entering the Kingdom can be done only gently, reverently, and with some laughter.*

My time alone was working in me like leavening.

But the rest of day five passed without the one thing I wanted most: a cure for my pain. No matter how much I tried to make sense out of this mystery of my own feminine nature, to heal myself, to wonder about God, I still felt as if I'd just delivered a ten-pound baby cactus covered with sharp, poisonous spines. And I was as tired as ever — so tired I'd been able to go for a walk only once in five days. Why wasn't I better? What was it I didn't know yet?

On my last night in Big Sur, I was dismal. I sat curled up on the couch in front of the window in my cabin, writing disconsolate words in my journal. By then, there seemed almost no chance my time in seclusion was going to result in the relief from pain I had sought. It was already 11:00 p.m.; I was heading home sometime the next morning. And I still had no solutions.

Sentences, paragraphs slowly filled the pages of my journal, words of melancholy and rumination — why wasn't I well? Where could I go from here? How long was it going to take to get well?

Suddenly, in midsentence, a dark possibility overtook me and stopped my pen: Maybe I was *never* going to be free of this exhausting pain. Maybe I was never going to be healthy again, never free of fatigue. Never — no matter what I did, no matter how much I needed relief, no matter how enlightened or "feminine" I might become. Once more I began to pour out troubling thoughts:

Here it is, the last night of my retreat, and I'm feeling low energy, really down. What's the truth for me now? I have loved being here at Big Sur, loved being alone, loved just being. I have not been afraid. I could not believe the hours and hours I was needing to do nothing . . . and I think I still need more hours. But I want to go home feeling well. I want to be UP, to make myself UP, to have experienced communion with God and come away a changed person.

I probably have come away changed — but not what I would call the right kind of change, not what my ego judges as the right kind of Ann. But the fact is I'm just the Ann I am. Right now this Ann is weary, sick, and in pain. I wish the peace I felt at times this week compensated for the weariness I live with. I don't know who I am anymore. I wanted to be upbeat, high energy, witty, funny, ON Ann when I left here. But I am so tired.

What scares me is if I do start to feel a lot better under thyroid treatment, it will be hard to keep myself from wanting to be that achiever again. Perhaps the key is balance. I was at one end of the spectrum; I'm now at the other. Maybe if I change and learn to be quiet, I won't be so tired. Maybe then I'd be a whole, peaceful, happy person.

But my Ego-Ann is a lot to give up! Though she gets me into trouble, she gets so much done, she's so showy and vivacious. But think of the expense, Ann — what it costs you in energy, appreciation and savoring of life, doctor bills! Is it worth it? The temptation is great. I feel like crying for my miserable old tap-dancing Ann. I feel like I've lost my life.

The moment I wrote those last seven words, my consciousness froze. I was struck by a cataclysmic revelation. The meaning of the biblical paradox of losing one's life to save it split wide open, cleaving my heart. I was so terrified my hands began to sweat and my shoulders felt as if they had unhinged in their sockets:

Oh, my God. Lose your life so you may save it. Is this what losing your life to save it means? Giving up everything? Oh, God. No. Don't ask this of me. I'm afraid. I can't give myself up. I'm afraid to give up everything. What will happen to me? I haven't had enough of the other side yet — peace, quiet,

*communion — to know it's worth dying for. Have I even
the vaguest hint? But if I knew what was on the other
side, it would not be a sacrifice or death . . . and it must
be. I am so afraid . . .*

To die to my dreams, to die to living a pain-free and
happy life, to die to any claim of how my life should be, to
say I would accept the worst life has to offer — it broke my
bones, it sucked the breath from my mouth. I could not
bear it. I cried as if on the brink of the dark, empty hole of
my own grave:

*I am mourning the death of good Old-Ann who enter-
tains, pleases, performs, throws energy carelessly every
which way, pushes, strives, achieves . . . and gets very
sick and further from herself. Who is Ann? I don't know.
I cry because I'm giving up everything for something
totally unknown — perhaps worth nothing, perhaps
someone "I" wouldn't even like. And I have no choice.
The choosing has already been done. I'm not walking
on in joy; it is into a dense cloud of the unknown. I cry
because I can't turn back, and I don't know where I'm
going.*

At that moment I was pulled under by a tidal wave of
emotion. I truly did not know what was going to happen to
me. The journal slid from my hands; my feelings overtook
me. The experience that followed was so powerful I could
not write about it until the following morning:

*After writing the words above, I cried and cried, mourned
my death, the death of Ann, the shell I'd created to*

stand for me. I saw this vaulting stone altar, the altar of God. Into the great bronze sacrificial bowl that rested on that altar I put everything I had, weeping over giving up my creativity, my health, my sense of humor, my wit, my talents, my body, my "pretty" face, my loved ones, my life, everything — and I raged at God.

I had tried to make me into something special, and people even liked it. I'd already had to give up so much in my depression. Now God wanted it all, to turn me into a dull, sick and in pain, nothing of a person. I cried and cried, in the end sacrificing everything, telling God to take it all and throw it on the bone wagon.

Then I saw a death cart come to the altar. As I wept, an angel voice whispered silently, "I know it's hard, but look where that Ann has gotten you, so sick and so tired." Spectral workers threw Ann on the death cart. But as they wheeled her away, I saw that she was only reflections in shattered pieces of mirror!

Had my Old-Ann been only an illusion? A trick done with mirrors? Not really me at all? In puzzlement and wonder, I laughed. What was I supposed to do now? "Here I am," I cried. "What is it you want to say to me, God?"

God said, "I am yours and you are mine."

Again, I was so astonished, I laughed. And I asked, "What do You get in that bargain?"

God laughed, and then replied, "A sense of humor!"

God liked my sense of humor! God, Life, Ultimate Reality, the Magnificently Creative Life Force needed, wanted, something — no, everything — I had thought of as mine.

There was more, much more, that night. For every tear I'd wept, now I laughed. On that night, I died, and was given a new life.

What might a group of psychoanalysts conclude about my experience if they'd been looking in on me that night? Would they have said I was being overdramatic or I was having a "spiritual emergency"? Would they have deemed it a spontaneous renunciation of the false-self, the death of the ego? Would they have called it a transforming experience, or a giving over to a new center, the true Self?

What would an interfaith group of clergy have said about my "dark night of the soul"? Would they have said I was imagining things? Would they have said I'd received a vision? Would they have pronounced me "saved"?

Whatever it was, in dying to my old life, in dying to the Old-Ann and her game plan, I had been given a new life, a life with a new direction.

What an amazing riddle, what a gift life is! I was at peace. Nothing had changed. I was still in pain. I still didn't have answers. I was still tired and not very well. But now I was committed to embracing whatever life brought me — and, more than that, I was committed to allowing myself to be transformed by it.

The next morning I packed up the car, but I was reluctant to leave my cloister. Delaying, I busied myself by double-checking for stray belongings around the cottage, but I knew there was some more important reason I was lingering there. Finally it came to me, what it was I was waiting for.

I went into the kitchen and ran a little water into a paper cup. The morning sun was just crawling up over the bannister of the deck, and I went out there and stood facing the woods. Holding the cup in my left hand, I dipped the fingertips of my right hand in the water. The drops clung there and trembled in the light. I took a breath, waited, and then touched the droplets to my head. It was my baptism, a ritual to symbolize my new life.

Minutes later, I locked the cabin, touching the door in a blessing for all that had happened there. I got in the car and drove to the lodge to drop off the key to the cabin. As I slid the cabin key across the counter, the woodsy-looking fellow behind the cash register looked at me, then looked again and said, "You sure have a pretty face." Grinning inwardly, I thanked him for his compliment. When I got in the car to leave, I caught a glimpse of myself in the rearview mirror and broke into delighted laughter because, when my eyes met mine, my first thought was, *Hey, God, that guy likes Your face!*

I drove back to civilization stunned, almost overwhelmed by the beauty that surrounded me — the hazy blue of the Pacific Ocean as I drove up the coast, giant redwoods pointing the way to heaven, and a Bach hymn building a cathedral of music all around me in my car.

When I got as far as the hot flats near Hollister, I started thinking about home. I remembered how beautiful it was, and I thought of Old-Ann, all put together with frayed nerve ends, wires, and mirrors — a robot-woman who had shopped, fixed, slaved, pushed, and shoved to create that house and everything in it. I drove with tears running down my cheeks, realizing I was going to inherit it from her — all of it. I felt so sorry for her, and blessed by grace to receive the beautiful place she had created — the old round deco mirror, the armoire, the bouquets of flowers, all those miniature angels, every little thing.

Then, in another wave of emotion, I realized I would inherit Larry, exquisite, extraordinary, loving Larry. She had found him, and now I got to live with him and love him the rest of my life. And John: Old-Ann had borne him in struggle, pain, and terror, and I got to receive him now, this glorious man-child, to love and adore for always.

The tears wouldn't stop but fell down my face as I drove home to the wonderful new life I had on a lease from God.

Yes, my pain was with me, too — my companion, pain, my taskmaster, and teacher. Life seemed beautifully complete. There was nowhere else I was supposed to be; life was only now, and now, and now again.

————

It was the end of a long journey and the beginning of a new one for me. When I returned from Big Sur, I had a new life and a heart full of mindful new questions:

Can I embrace my continuing pain, find the blessing in it, and be transformed by it?

What does it really mean to be a woman?

If the power of the feminine comes from being, not doing, what does it mean to "be"?

How will my life be different if I don't measure it out in tasks, but in the moment-by-moment experience of being?

How can I help Duke and Valentine successfully coexist?

*Can I continue my solitary religious journey, find ways to
grow spiritually, learn to deepen my understanding, and
love more?*

Now, more than two years later, I am awed by what is
happening to me. Each day of my life I awaken a little more
to the person I might be, to the sun-and-moon, night-and-
day difference between *being* and *doing.* What a difference
this is making in me, in Duke and in Valentine. In active
imagination I see the two of them now:

> *I go down a long hall to find Valentine. I come upon her
> in a dome-shaped room filled with flowers; the walls of
> the room are quilted with the same cream-colored satin
> as the dress Valentine is now wearing. Though this is still
> a sick room, Valentine looks healthier and much less
> sad.*
>
> *I am worried about Valentine, though, because the
> room seems too brightly lit by the sun. When I share my
> concern with her, she smiles and presses a button as her
> reply. Slowly the floor lowers until we are in an enor-
> mous, dark underground cavern. I look to my left and
> see Valentine, now in a simple garment of blue home-
> spun, kneeling in front of a great altar flanked by
> candles. A cross hangs above. For a time we are quiet.
> Then, together, we climb huge steps carved in the
> cavern's wall until we are back in Valentine's room
> again. I realize it is not sunlight that fills Valentine's
> room, but the light she brings back with her from below.*
>
> *When I invite Duke into Valentine's dome-shaped
> room, he comes in a changed man. Duke looks like a
> young artist, with his hair tousled, worn long and curly*

now. Instead of his former bad-ass black, Duke wears a
soft dark shirt, blue jeans, and work boots. His face is
gentler, softer, though not completely trustworthy yet.
I look at Valentine and see by her face how vulner-
able she will always be to his opinions. I know I will
always have to monitor Duke in order to protect Valen-
tine and the values she holds for me. As Duke leaves us
and walks down the long hall, I catch a phantom vision
of him in the distant future wearing the garments of a
priest.

What I am living is a reconciliation of my own masculine and feminine values. What I am finding is my own
wholeness. As I learn to recognize the *doing* habits that
once ran my life, I gain the power to benefit from the
initiative and drive my Duke-side has always given me,
without allowing that drive to use me. As I learn to give
greater credence to the feminine value of *being*, once held
in secret trust for me by Valentine, I gain the freedom to
make healthier, more rewarding, more creative choices,
and my life sends down roots deeper and deeper into
meaning.

When I find I'm caught up in my old task orientation
— hurriedly crashing through housework, writing, errands,
meal preparation, laundry, whatever, just to chalk each
item off my list — I know Duke, my do-er, has taken power.
And I deliberately slow down and concentrate on one thing
at a time. When I'm *doing*, what's next always seems more
important than now. And the truth is, the pleasure of life
cannot be experienced anywhere *but* now.

During these past two years, I've also learned that my
Duke is a great admirer of efficiency. Now, when I feel

myself gearing up to knock down a line of tasks like domi-
nos all in a row, warning sirens go off in my head. I might
be on my way home from the library; it's way past lunch,
and I'm tired and hungry. Yet I'll suddenly find myself
plotting out an "efficient" plan for stopping at the grocery
before I go home . . . and I could pick up those stamps I
need at the post office right after that . . . and then swing
by the gas station . . . and there's a sale on socks at . . .
Warning! Warning! Warning!

"Oh no you don't, Duke," I say to myself. I make
myself slow down, go home, eat lunch, and then decide
what *really* needs to be taken care of that day.

Ironically, one of the places I'm most vulnerable to the
seduction of Duke's efficiency is in my own kitchen, where
I easily fall into my old habit of juggling several tasks at
once — emptying the dishwasher, talking on the phone
with the receiver pinched between my ear and shoulder,
and stirring up a pot of chili at the same time. I see Duke's
hand in such "efficiencies" now. While I value the strength
and drive Duke, my inner man, gives me, I cannot let him
take me over. There is no pleasure in his blind *doing*. The
days I revert to *doing* are as jarring and jolting as roller-
skating on boulders.

On the other hand, when I think of Valentine and
remember to *be*, the days feel as soothing as waltzing on
new-fallen leaves and pine needles. When I practice the
feminine value of *being*, my life feels deeper, calmer, more
earthy and satisfying. In *being*, I am slowly learning to give
myself over to the appreciation of whatever I am involved
with at the moment. For its own sake. I pick yellowed
leaves off the geraniums not to cross this job off my list, but
to pick yellowed leaves off the geraniums, for the entirety
of that experience: the scarlet flower petals, the baked

surface of the clay pots, the velvety green leaves, the papery yellow leaves, the peppery perfume left on my hands, even the dirt caught under my fingernails.

When I'm *being,* no task is more important than any other task. Each moment is full of unexpected rewards for my senses, my mind, and emotions. I still accomplish all of the same tasks I used to. The difference is, when I *be,* my life seems to glow quietly from within like a numinous paper lantern. In *being,* I embrace life at its essence — not just its "good" and "lofty" moments, but every passionately human, painful, ordinary, beautiful, vibrating moment.

———

Being with Time:
When I remember to *be* with my time, I settle into my life's own rhythms like a comfy pair of shoes. In *being,* I am discovering how much I need and value quiet time, how much better I feel when I take time to read; time to think; time to sit on the swing in the afternoons, rocking — just for the sake of that gentle, going-nowhere movement; just for the sake of watching the way the poplar trees ceaselessly rustle and flash their tiny leaf-fans in the sunlight overhead.

Being with My Body:
When I remember to *be,* I am more likely to listen to and heed my body's whispered requests. How much more healthful and satisfying food is when I choose what my body wants and needs, rather than what is fastest and most portable. How blessed it is to give in to my fatigue and curl up under the afghan for a twenty-minute nap on a weary afternoon. How natural it seems to go to bed at night when my internal clock winds down, instead of waiting until the

clock on the wall strikes eleven. I may never be able to make my fatigue and pain go away, but *being* helps.

Being with My Work:
Do I miss the big-time daily grind? Well, maybe a little. But I have no desire to live like that again. Now, when I remember to *be*, I am not a slave to my work, but a participant in the act of creation. On the days I am able to *be*, I write not to get to the end of a chapter, to reach a goal, to put another hash mark on the wall, to watch the pages pile up, but for the experience of writing itself — for the love of words and ideas, rather than applause or a paycheck. Now, when my creative well is dry, I don't write, I *be*, and I am amazed to find that soon the well is full to overflowing once again.

Being with Relationships:
When I remember to *be*, it nurtures a gentle wisdom that cradles life. Recently, a neighbor stopped by, saying she just wanted to drop off a book. Out of *being*, I heard all that and felt there was something more. Minutes after she left, I went to her home and knocked on her door. When she saw me, she burst into tears. "What can I do?" I wanted to know. We could talk. And we did. Then, because she was too upset to drive, I took her to her doctor's appointment. When I *be*, I am no longer too busy or too preoccupied to read the subtle, or not so subtle, signs friends and loved ones use to telegraph their needs.

Even Larry senses a deep change in me. On two separate evenings, after I'd had particularly *being* afternoons, Larry came home, walked up behind me as I was putting the finishing touches on dinner, and leaned down to kiss my neck. "Wow," he said, slightly awed, "You're so soft." And I know where that softness comes from. It's more than skin deep; it's a softness that comes from being more quiet at the center. It is Valentine's wisdom and softness that allow me to notice and respond to another person's needs in just the way I am learning to notice and respond to my own.

Being with God:
What is the nature of God? What is love? What is God's will? What is life asking of me? What is my spiritual expression? I am only a beginner, but I feel I am finally on a path worth following. For the most part, I need a solitary journey centered on daily quiet time, which may include prayer, journal writing, poetry, recording my dreams, singing hymns, or studying scriptures and ideas from our great world heritage of religion and psychology. I also count myself fortunate to have found a Jungian therapist with whom I can share my inner journey, making the life of the spirit even more abundantly rich and deeply moving.

The words I sang in Big Sur are still the words that guide my days: "Breathe on me, Breath of God, Fill me with life anew, That I may love what Thou dost love, And do what Thou wouldst do." For now I know that my will must be for the most creative response to life, for the greatest good, over and over again in every moment of the day.

Being with Doing:
I am discovering that every moment, no matter how seemingly mundane, holds the vibrancy of life, if I will only *be* with it. There is a difference between cooking to get a meal on the table or simply over with, and cooking for the experience of cooking. The feel of a sharp knife, tsh-ing through an onion ... the onion's translucent whiteness and pungent eye-smarting aroma as it falls into a dice on a

well-grooved cutting board . . . the rich homey smell of that onion browning in a heavy pan . . . the flavor of that onion mingled with wine and butter, chicken and herbs when it's later in my mouth. Ah, life lived this way — I could eat it with a spoon, drink it up from a cup!

And sometimes, when I step outside just to *be* with the evening, I suddenly find the air so exquisite and silvery beautiful that breathing it, living this one ordinary life, thrills me with pure and ecstatic wonder.

———

Yes, my pain still carves me. Yes, I still despise it. Sometimes I still feel hopeless and desperate at having to bear it one more day and one more day again. But, because I must, I do. I continue to "practice" the gymnast's iron cross, grasping equally onto the twin rings of hope for better health and complete acceptance of my health as it is now.

Through it all, I know this intolerable, despised pain is my own. It belongs to me, was made for me, and is a blessing in my life. In my secret heart I know this wound has been my healing. I believe it may always be so — that it is our wounds, our very wounds, that heal us.

I do not mean to ennoble pain and suffering. There is no nobility in suffering, only in what we do with it. If we allow it, suffering will embitter us, shrivel us to vile, poisonous people. If we allow it, suffering becomes an excuse to lash out at life, to withdraw from the world and wear the hairshirt of victimization. But it does not have to be so. We may, instead, choose to *use* our suffering to make us more whole, more real, and more human. Suffering and pain are blessings only to the extent that we allow them to transform our lives for the good.

Soren Kierkegaard has written:

> For affliction recruits hope. It does not bestow hope, but it recruits it. . . . For affliction prevents [a person] mercilessly from obtaining any other help or relief whatsoever; affliction compels him mercilessly to let go of everything else; affliction schools him mercilessly, schools him thoroughly, that he may learn to grasp the eternal and to hold on to the eternal. Affliction does not help directly, it is not affliction that acquires or purchases hope and makes a present of it to a man; it helps repellently, and can do no otherwise, because hope is in man himself. Affliction preaches awakening.[7]

Affliction has awakened me, has recruited hope and joy where I least expected it. Suffering has taken me down to bedrock, and there I have found new meaning for my life. Would I take back that experience if I could? If I could make my years of depression and pain magically disappear, would I? I would not. I value, above all, the harvest that has come from this rocky, thorny ground. But I dream:

> *I am alone. Suddenly, unseen, a bolt of laser-light strikes my body. Unearthly power blasts through me, setting every cell spinning. I throw my hands up in fear and wonder, as I shout, "I am being healed!" I know that I am. Maybe not this moment. Maybe not tomorrow. But I am being healed of my pain.*

For eight years I have wrestled my Dark Angel, in the depths of depression and in the glass-shard fields of pain. I have fought the Angel with all my mind, all my soul, and all my strength. I have never, never let go. And this one thing I know: My Dark Angel has blessed me.

———

Only Now

Nothing matters
except
this
one
omnipotent moment.
Now.

Not gold-plated achievements,
nor dreams
for the future,
nor nightmares
of the past.

All that matters
is everything.
Everything
in this one moment,
this one,
now . . .

. . . this icy silver rain
staccato against my windowpane

. . . this darkening
and dazzle of winter sun
shimmering in those
particular pines

. . . this springtime windowbox,
singing in my eyes, a gaudy,
flirtation of flowers

. . . this baby's bottom powdered,
silken smooth, like well-kneaded
bread dough beneath my blissful hand

. . . this coughing-coin laughter
that catches, bursts, and soars,
and gilds the room with joy

. . . this splashing, glass-shard pain,
this urgent message of life
from body to brain

. . . this hairy, crawling
fear-creature now alive
and let loose in my belly

. . . this white-hot anger
spewing from the blast furnace
of my hate

. . . *this cold, gray shroud*
of grief descending to cocoon
or ensnare me in my loss

. . . *this achingly bittersweat*
good-bye to a grown son who will
return to us only as a guest

. . . *this one man's arms*
circling me with extraordinary love,
cradling me against his chest

. . . *this flannel comfort bed*
tight-tucked with fragrant sheets
fresh from the dryer

. . . *this toothy, orange crunch*
of carrot I've finally
removed from the end of my stick

> *leaving me only*
> *with this*
> *one,*
> *richly abundant,*
> *omnipotent*
> *moment.*
> *Now.*

Notes

1. Judith Duerk, *CIRCLE OF STONES: Woman's Journey To Herself* (San Diego: LuraMedia, 1989), 36.

2. National Mental Health Association.

3. Duerk, 40. Duerk uses the lower case "s" in the word "self" to indicate the finite sense of self within the individual, already in the child, which will later form a relationship with the transcendent, or infinite, Self. (Based on the works of C. G. Jung.)

4. Ibid, 31.

5. Ibid, 40.

6. Thomas P. Beresford, M.D.; Richard DeVaul, M.D.; Earl R. Gardner, Ph.D.; Anne K. Hall, C.R.N.A.; Richard C. W. Hall, M.D.; Michael K. Popkin, M.D.; "Psychiatric Manifestations of Hashimoto's Thyroiditis," *Psychosomatics* (April 1982): 337.

7. Soren Kierkegaard, *CHRISTIAN DISCOURSES*, translated by Walter Lowrie. (London: Oxford University Press, 1939).

The Author

Photograph by John Robert Keiffer

Ann grew up in a small town in the heartland of Ohio. She graduated from Ashland University, where she was a member of the English Department's Honors Seminar. Though Ann has loved words all her life, she was thirty-four before she named her passion and made writing her career. Completely self-taught in the field of advertising, she launched a business as a free-lance advertising copywriter. A year-and-a-half later, she was hired by a division of one of the world's most prestigious advertising agencies.

Ann and her husband, Larry, live in San Mateo, California, where Ann is currently at work on her second book and the rest of her life.

LuraMedia Publications

BANKSON, MARJORY ZOET
Braided Streams: *Esther and a Woman's Way of Growing*
Seasons of Friendship: *Naomi and Ruth as a Pattern*

BOHLER, CAROLYN STAHL
Prayer on Wings: *A Search for Authentic Prayer*

BOZARTH, ALLA RENEE
Womanpriest: *A Personal Odyssey (Revised Edition)*

GEIGER, LURA JANE
Astonish Me, Yahweh Leader's Guide

and PATRICIA BACKMAN
Braided Streams Leader's Guide

and SUSAN TOBIAS
Seasons of Friendship Leader's Guide

and SANDY LANDSTEDT, MARY GECKELER, PEGGIE OURY
Astonish Me, Yahweh!: *A Bible Workbook-Journal*

JEVNE, RONNA FAY
It All Begins With Hope: *Patients, Caretakers, and the Bereaved Speak Out*

and ALEXANDER LEVITAN
No Time for Nonsense: *Getting Well Against the Odds*

KEIFFER, ANN
Gift of the Dark Angel: *A Woman's Journey through Depression toward Wholeness*

LODER, TED
Eavesdropping on the Echoes: *Voices from the Old Testament*
Guerrillas of Grace: *Prayers for the Battle*
No One But Us: *Personal Reflections on Public Sanctuary*
Tracks in the Straw: *Tales Spun from the Manger*
Wrestling the Light: *Ache and Awe in the Human-Divine Struggle*

LUCIANI, JOSEPH
Healing Your Habits: *Introducing Directed Imagination, A Successful Technique for Overcoming Addictive Problems*

MCMAKIN, JACQUELINE
with SONYA DYER
Working from the Heart: *For Those Who Search for Meaning and Satisfaction in Their Work*

MEYER, RICHARD C.
One Anothering: *Biblical Building Blocks for Small Groups*

MILLETT, CRAIG
In God's Image: *Archetypes of Women in Scripture*

O'CONNOR, ELIZABETH
Cry Pain, Cry Hope *(Revised Edition)*
Search for Silence *(Revised Edition)*

SCHAPER, DONNA
A Book of Common Power: *Narratives Against the Current*
Stripping Down: *The Art of Spiritual Restoration*

WEEMS, RENITA J.
Just a Sister Away: *A Womanist Vision of Women's Relationships in the Bible*

LuraMedia Women's Series

BORTON, JOAN
Drawing from the Women's Well: *Reflections from the Life Passage of Menopause*

CARTLEDGE-HAYES, MARY
To Love Delilah: *Claiming the Women of the Bible*

DAHL, JUDY
River of Promise: *Two Women's Story of Love and Adoption*

DUERK, JUDITH
Circle of Stones: *Woman's Journey to Herself*

RUPP, JOYCE
The Star in My Heart: *Experiencing Sophia, Inner Wisdom*

SCHAPER, DONNA
Superwoman Turns 40: *The Story of One Woman's Intentions to Grow Up*

LuraMedia, Inc. , 7060 Miramar Rd., Suite 104, San Diego, CA 92121
Books for Healing and Hope, Balance and Justice.